TERENCE CAVE
"Far other worlds, and other seas":
Thinking with Literature in the Twenty-First Century

17 October 2014, University of Berne, Main Building (Auditorium Maximum)

Fondazione
Internazionale Balzan
"Premio"

Akademien der Wissenschaften Schweiz
Académies suisses des sciences
Accademie svizzere delle scienze
Academias svizras da las scienzas
Swiss Academies of Arts and Sciences

Accademia Nazionale dei Lincei

THE ANNUAL BALZAN LECTURE

6

"FAR OTHER WORLDS, AND OTHER SEAS"

Thinking with Literature in the Twenty-First Century

by

TERENCE CAVE

2009 Balzan Prizewinner

LEO S. OLSCHKI

2015

CASA EDITRICE LEO S. OLSCHKI
Viuzzo del Pozzetto, 8
50126 Firenze
www.olschki.it

ISBN 978 88 222 6407 7

CONTENTS

ALBERTO QUADRIO CURZIO

Vice President of the International Balzan Foundation "Prize",
President of the Class of Moral, Historical and Philological Sciences of the
Accademia Nazionale dei Lincei

FOREWORD

The Sixth Annual Balzan Lecture, delivered by Terence Cave, can be regarded as another landmark for the Balzan Foundation. This distinguished lecture series continues to stand as a vital testimonial to the ongoing collaboration between the Swiss Academies of Arts and Sciences, the Accademia Nazionale dei Lincei and the Balzan Foundation and their efforts to open an arena for Balzan Prizewinners to give the public a privileged view of their careers and present issues and findings related to the Balzan Research Projects. Moreover, the series also underlines the Balzan Foundation's fundamental role in fostering communication between the sciences and the humanities at the highest level of international scholarship.

On this occasion, I am honoured to write the foreword to the sixth volume in this masterfully constructed set of contributions to contemporary academic discourse in all disciplines, and I am also pleased that our carefully meditated efforts in promoting this initiative have been successful in making it possible to bring the unsurpassed achievements of the Balzan Prizewinners to the attention of a wider audience.

To briefly outline the published series of lectures, the first volume presented the results of Peter and Rosemary Grant's research project involving young academics on the seminal topic of *The Evolution of Darwin's Finches, Mockingbirds and Flies.* The second lecture by Anthony Grafton, entitled *Humanists with Inky Fingers. The Culture of Correction in Renaissance Europe,* provided a detailed analysis of the impact of these correctors on the meaning of the texts they were working on. The third lecture by Colin Renfrew illustrated the findings from his excavations on the Greek island of Keros in the project *Cognitive Archaeology from Theory to Practice*. Michael Marmot delivered the fourth lecture, *Fair Society, Healthy Lives*, in which he examined the social determinants of health. Last year, Kurt Lambeck's lecture, entitled *Of Moon and Land, Ice and Strand: Sea Level during Glacial Cycles*, offered a very timely contribution to the debate on the consequences of human impact on the Earth as well as to the very long cycles of changes in the world's physical structure.

Today's lecture, *"Far other worlds, and other seas": Thinking with Literature in the Twenty-First Century*, will be delivered by Terence Cave, whose brilliant career devoted to teaching and research in the field of modern French literature has resulted in fundamental contributions to a new understanding of Renaissance literature and the influence of Aristotelian poetics in modern European literature, as acknowledged in the motivation for his 2009 Balzan Prize for Literature since 1500. Part of the award has been used to create the Balzan Interdisciplinary Seminar 'Literature as an Object of Knowledge' at the St. John's College Research Centre at Oxford, which marks the new direction he has embarked upon to find ways of integrating cognitive research into mainstream readings of literature.

WELCOME ADDRESS BY MARTIN TÄUBER

President of the University of Berne

Esteemed guests,
Ladies and gentlemen,
Honoured Balzan Lecturer Professor Terence Cave,
Dear colleagues,

It is my great pleasure and a privilege to welcome you all to the 2014 Balzan Lecture here in the Auditorium Maximum of the University of Berne. The auditorium is located in the main building of the University, which was completed in the year 1903, at the time when the University of Berne started its development in the Länggasse Quartier. From this location, the University overlooks the city of Berne, the Federal Building, and from here one can – on clear days – enjoy the majestic range of the Bernese Alps. This location is of course also an inspiration, reminding us of our location at the political and administrative centre of Switzerland as well as the importance of the environment, of nature and of infrastructure.

We are proud and excited that the organizers, in particular the Swiss Academies of Arts and Sciences, have chosen this venue for today's celebration. While the first impression of the main building may suggest that you are entering an institution that has come of age and lost touch with modern life, the opposite is true. The University of Berne is a dynamic, growing and successful university. All major scientific areas are taught and developed at our university, with the sole exception of engineering sciences. We are proud of a number of centres of excellence in research and teaching, which range from climate sciences to medicine and veterinary medicine, biology, physics and astrophysics, law, economy, social sciences, theology and of course – very much at the centre tonight – the wide fields of the humanities. In all these areas, a special emphasis is placed on interdisciplinary approaches and a strong drive to support sustainable solutions and strategies.

Only through the free exchange of ideas and the contribution of all disciplines of science can we hope to broaden and further develop the collective knowledge of humanity. This is certainly necessary to successfully confront the challenges that we face today in so many areas. As examples of such challenges, let me just mention not only the environment and the climate, but also the many conflicts and political instabilities throughout the globe.

With this short introduction, it is my pleasure to hand over the podium to Professor Enrico Decleva, President of the International Balzan Foundation "Prize".

OPENING REMARKS BY ENRICO DECLEVA

President of the International Balzan Foundation "Prize"

It is a great honour and pleasure to be here for the first time as President of the Balzan Foundation "Prize" to introduce an Annual Balzan Lecture. First and foremost, I would like to thank everyone who has worked together and made such a great effort to make this an important event for the Foundation and the Balzan Prize. Let me start with Professor Quadrio Curzio, who unfortunately cannot be with us today. He is the "patron" of the formula for collaboration between the Balzan Foundation, the Swiss Academies of Arts and Sciences and the Accademia Nazionale dei Lincei, which accentuates the Italo-Swiss nature of the Balzan Prize and its multi-disciplinary inspiration. In addition, for his enthusiastic support in this endeavour, I would also like to thank the President of the Swiss Academies of Arts and Sciences, Thierry Courvoisier, who has taken up the baton from former President Peter Suter, now member of the Balzan General Prize Committee. And my thanks to the Rector of the University of Berne, Martin Täuber, for the hospitality always shown when the Foundation is there. The Balzan Prize is at home in Berne, carrying out the awards ceremony at the Federal Palace and the Prizewinners Forum at the Swiss National Science Foundation, so being guests in the city's Athenaeum also gives us an even greater sense of belonging.

The Italo-Swiss collaboration underlying the Annual Balzan Lecture enhances the international nature of the Prize and the Balzan Foundation by intertwining different cultures. It is our strongest trait, and one which also distinguishes Professor Terence Cave, whom we will listen to shortly and whom I thank for agreeing to accept our invitation. Terence Cave was awarded the 2009 Balzan Prize for Literature since 1500 *for his outstanding contributions to a new understanding of Renaissance literature and of the influence of Aristotelian poetics in modern European literature.* The *laudatio* that accompanies this motivation states that he succeeded in showing how the rhetorical concept of *copia*, or abundance, can be considered a fundamental element in the sixteenth century Renaissance. And there is more. In his works, Cave has revealed the profound bonds that link the rediscovery of Aristotelian poetics in the course of the Italian Renaissance to modern forms of drama and the novel, as well as to theoretical reflections on poetry at the end of the twentieth century. Thus, his work is distinguished by a broad European horizon and a profound historical perspective, and these characteristics make Professor Cave a scholar who tries to break down – or at least look beyond – certain disciplinary barriers. It gives me pleasure to underline this because these are the qualities that the Balzan Prize tries to discover and highlight both in the humanities as well as in the experimental sciences.

INTRODUCTION BY THIERRY COURVOISIER

President of the Swiss Academies of Arts and Sciences

A very warm welcome to all of you tonight, also in the name of the Swiss Academies of Arts and Sciences. It is a great pleasure to be host to the Annual Balzan Lecture in Berne this year. It takes us out of our daily routine for the pleasure of a high quality intellectual and inter-disciplinary exercise, as for some of us French literature by British experts is not part of our daily bread.

Thus, many thanks to the Balzan Foundation for allowing us to have the lecture here and co-organizing it with us, and many thanks to all those who have indeed made this event possible. It is a great plea-sure to welcome the distinguished British scholar Terence Cave, who has devoted most of his life to French literature and to teaching the same subject. It is a particular pleasure for me, a long-time admirer of Montaigne – his doubts and his very special, possibly unique way of writing – to introduce our lecturer, although I have just been told that we will not hear anything about Montaigne in the coming hour.

In any event, I am very much looking forward to listening to you, Professor Cave, but first, let's learn something about you from Thomas Claviez.

PRESENTATION OF TERENCE CAVE
BY THOMAS CLAVIEZ

Professor of Literary Theory, Co-director of the Center for Cultural Studies and
Director of the MA Programme "World Literature" at the University of Berne

It is a great pleasure and an extraordinary honour to introduce to
you Professor Terence Cave, Professor Emeritus of French Literature,
as well as Emeritus Research Fellow at Oxford University and Honorary Fellow at Caius College, Cambridge, who will deliver the 2014
Balzan Lecture. The Center for Cultural Studies and the Philosophi-
cal-Historical Faculty of the University of Berne are truly honoured to
host this lecture, in cooperation with the International Balzan Foundation and the Swiss Academies of the Arts and Sciences.

In the rather tight time slot that I have been allotted to introduce
both Professor Terence Cave and our distinguished respondent, Professor Elleke Boehmer, also from Oxford University, I cannot claim to
do adequate justice to Professor Cave's oeuvre, which spans 45 years of
intellectual life, and several hundred centuries of subject matter. This
oeuvre has its beginnings with his book *Devotional Poetry in France
1570-1613*, which was followed, a decade later, by his monograph *The
Cornucopian Text: Problems of Writing in the French Renaissance*, a
book that established him as one of the leading Renaissance scholars
in Europe. He subsequently broadened his perspective to engage with
the history of poetics. In 1988, his book *Recognitions: A Study in Poetics* was published, which has since become a reference work on this
topic, following, as it does, the concept of *anagnorisis* from Aristotle
up to the twentieth century. This concept – besides *peripeteia* and *pa-
thos* – plays a key role in the latter's *Poetics*. Among the many books
that have followed, I would like to mention *How To Read Montaigne*
(2007), which succeeds, in a unique manner, in on the one hand root-
ing Montaigne's essays firmly in his time and historical context, but at
the same time making them speak to us in a fresh and contemporary

manner. Professor Cave has also published in French. Thus, his two-volume *Pré-histoires: Textes troubles au seuil de la modernité* (1999 and 2001) successfully transposed into the French literary context an approach that has become known as New Historicism. Among his most fascinating books, however, is his 2011 *Mignon's Afterlife: Crossing Cultures from Goethe to the Twenty-First Century*, which traces the exceptional history and literary career of this mysterious and androgynous female character, who enters the scene of Goethe's *Wilhelm Meisters Lehrjahre* as part of a faring group of acrobats, jugglers and wire dancers. Offspring of an incestuous relationship (at this point unknown to her parents, Harfner, a slightly deranged ballad-monger, and his sister Sperata, who will later go mad and die), Mignon becomes a mixture between muse and servant for Wilhelm Meister. Once Meister proposes to Therese in front of Mignon's eyes, she dies immediately of a broken heart, but will continue to haunt and preoccupy the fantasies of many more artists to come.

Terence Cave follows the remarkable artistic afterlife of this arcane figure, as Mignon steps out of the shadow of Wilhelm and fashions a destiny of her own. She becomes the object of an obsessive interest that reached its peak in the later nineteenth century, but continues to reverberate into the twenty-first century. She reappears – often as a character bearing a different name but sharing an unmistakable family resemblance with her – in a wide range of different literary and musical works from Goethe via the German romantic novel, Mme de Staël, George Sand, Nerval and Baudelaire, Walter Scott and George Eliot to Gerhart Hauptmann and Angela Carter.

Professor Cave uses this opportunity in an ingenious way to show his readers how different facets of this unique figure are foregrounded and reverberate in, as they are adapted by, distinct literary eras and generic contexts. I would like to quote critic David Baguley here, who has described this book as follows:

> In this delightfully informative, leisurely, and sophisticated study, Terence Cave traces the multiple re-embodiments of a relatively minor character from Goethe's *Wilhelm Meisters Lehrjahre*. The scope of the investigation is impressively broad, spanning more than two centuries and covering the English, French, and German cultures in particular, with occasional references to other traditions such as that of the early Mignon precursor, the *gitanilla* figure in Spain. An extraordinary array of major and minor writers and artists is shown to have dallied with the tantalizing and ubiquitous figure of this adolescent

girl, with her acrobatic skills, her dancing flair, and her musical talent, notably when she sings the hauntingly lyrical ballad "Kennst du das Land".[1]

– the land where the lemons bloom: the ballad that many commentators have identified as an early indication of Goethe's fascination with Italy.

If there is a common thread to be identified in Professor Cave's oeuvre – and I think this is what characterizes an outstanding scholar – then it is his passion to show his readers that literature opens a different access to the world; or, maybe, an access to different worlds, and I guess this is something we might want to come back to in the discussion that I will have the pleasure to moderate. In addition to his monographs, I would like to mention a book that he edited, which carries the title *Thomas More's* Utopia *in Early Modern Europe: Paratexts and Contexts* (2008). This edition provides the first complete account of all the editions of *Utopia*, whether vernacular or Latin, printed before 1650, together with a transcription of all the prefatory materials they contain. In addition, he has also translated Madame de Lafayette's *La Princesse de Clèves, La Princesse de Montpensier* and *La Comtesse de Tende* for Oxford World Classics.

I have already referred to his book *Recognitions*, a term which, needless to say, evokes another one, that of cognition. While **re**cognition [sic] is a highly charged, political term, the concept of cognition is situated rather in the fields of epistemology or the natural sciences. Taking together the questions whether what literature offers is a different access to the world, and the difference between recognition and cognition, we arrive at a third one: namely, whether literature is the subject at hand, or whether literature, in turn, offers us an opening to another subject: that of the world.

Which, indeed, brings us back to tonight's occasion, and the title of his talk. When, in 2009, Terence Cave was awarded the Balzan Prize for his outstanding scholarship on the Renaissance – and, as we have seen, way beyond – he decided to use this prize to establish the Balzan Interdisciplinary Seminar "Literature as an Object of Knowledge", which since has produced some outstanding young

---

[1] DAVID BAGULEY, "Mignon's Afterlives: Crossing Cultures from Goethe to the Twenty-First Century" (review), *French Studies: A Quarterly Review. 66:4 (October 2012)*: 592-593; 593.

scholars amongst its ranks. The seminar has set itself the task to "explore the value of literature as an object of knowledge and, more specifically, the cognitive value of literature in relation to other kinds of discourse". These lines allow for both interpretations: literature as an "object of knowledge", as well as a medium that generates, in turn, a certain knowledge about something outside of itself. In his statements on the reception of this distinguished award, Professor Cave specified his plans about this seminar as follows:

> Literature, I hope you will agree, is not merely a pleasure to be indulged in when one has nothing better to do. Because it embodies the most complex and imaginative uses of human language, it is an indispensable instrument of thought; it provides us with alternative ways of understanding the world and ourselves.

This I take as a move to liberate literature from the golden cage of contemplation, or disinterested interest that a certain Kantian variety of aesthetics has enclosed it in for more than 250 years; or, at least, to severely challenge the role it has enjoyed in the aftermath of Kant's dictum. It might indeed take a certain disinterest – and maybe the contemplative attitude to muster said disinterest – in order to disentangle ourselves from the glamour and the clamour of the political, economic and social (and thoroughly mediatized) world that surrounds us; a disentanglement required to reconnect us to the basic questions of humanity and human existence – and the environment we inhabit as such creatures – that are all but drowned out by discourses and regimes that, although product of our makings, sometimes seem to swallow us alive. Literature, and the unique cognitive strategies it features and activates, might serve to familiarize us with the unfamiliar, as well as – in a more modern take on it – to defamiliarize us with the automated perception of the seemingly familiar, as Viktor Shklovsky has argued.[2] It might thus bring us closer to the "far other worlds, and other seas", which the title of Professor Cave's talk tonight alludes to; it might also open up such other worlds right in our midst, in offering said alternative cognition mentioned above.

---

[2] VIKTOR SHKLOVSKY, "Art as Technique", in *Russian Formalist Criticism: Four Essays*, eds. Lee T. Lemon and Marion J. Reiss (Lincoln, University of Nebraska Press, 1965): 3-24.

The 2009 Balzan Prize is, however, by far not the only award Terence Cave has received for his scientific oeuvre and intellectual achievements. As you have already gathered from tonight's program, he is a member of the Academia Europaea (since 1990). He is Fellow of the British Academy (since 1991), Member of the Royal Norwegian Society of Science and Letters in Trondheim (since 1993), Chevalier dans l'Ordre National du Mérite (since 2001), and he was made Commander of the Order of the British Empire in 2013.

The "far other worlds, and other seas" are also the object of inquiry of our distinguished respondent to Terence Cave, Professor Elleke Boehmer, who – and I'd like to express our gratitude about that – has agreed to comment upon Professor Cave's talk, and whom I would like to welcome on this occasion as well. Besides their joint interest in "far other worlds", what Professors Cave and Boehmer share is their Alma Mater, Oxford University, where Elleke Boehmer is Professor of World Literature in English. She is also a Professorial Governing Body Fellow at Wolfson College. She is an acclaimed novelist and a founding figure in the field of Postcolonial Studies, and internationally recognized for her research in colonial and postcolonial literature and theory – an academic field that, I guess is safe to say, the Renaissance and its explorations and explorers have had their share in bequeathing upon us. As, again, you can gather from the invitation, Professor Boehmer is as prodigious a writer as is Professor Cave; her books include both scientific works as well as novels. Among the former, I would like to mention *Colonial and Postcolonial Literature* (1995), *Empire, the National and the Postcolonial, 1890-1920* (2002), *Stories of Women* (2005) and the biography *Nelson Mandela* (2008). She is, as I mentioned, also the author of four novels, including *Screens again the Sky* (short-listed David Hyam Prize, 1990), *Bloodlines* (short-listed SANLAM prize) and *Nile Baby* (2008), as well as the short-story collection *Sharmilla and Other Portraits* (2010). She has edited numerous collections that have become indispensable sources in the field of Postcolonial Studies. Furthermore, she is the General Editor of the Oxford Studies in Postcolonial Literatures Series.

She is thus uniquely qualified to serve as a respondent to Terence Cave in order to assess whether, and in what way, literature is either the object of cognition or the medium to offer a different kind of cognitive space – or, indeed, both. However, before we might tackle these, and probably many other questions that pertain to the world – or the worlds – of literature in the discussion that I will have the pleasure to moderate, please join me in welcoming Professor Terence Cave, the 2009 Balzan Prizewinner, who will deliver the 2014 Annual Balzan Lecture with the title "'Far other worlds, and other seas': Thinking with Literature in the Twenty-First Century."

Lecture by TERENCE CAVE

"FAR OTHER WORLDS, AND OTHER SEAS": THINKING WITH LITERATURE IN THE TWENTY-FIRST CENTURY

Good evening, ladies and gentlemen. It's wonderful to be back in this beautiful city on a beautiful day, just five years after I was here with my family through the generosity of the Balzan Foundation to receive the Prize. It was literally an awesome occasion, and it's a special pleasure for me to have the opportunity to refresh that memory.

I am honoured and delighted to give this year's Balzan Lecture, and I want first to express my deep gratitude to the International Balzan Prize Foundation, through its President Professor Decleva, for all the support they have given me during those five years. I am grateful also to the Swiss Academies of Arts and Sciences, its President, Professor Courvoisier, and its General Secretary, Dr. Markus Zürcher, who invited me to speak here; to the University of Berne, its President Professor Täuber and its Center for Cultural Studies, for hosting the lecture. Above all, I'm deeply indebted to the Center's co-director, Professor Thomas Claviez, for integrating this somewhat outlandish lecture into his programme and for introducing me so eloquently. And let me add a special word of thanks to Dr. Marlène Iseli, the Center's *wissenschaftliche Mitarbeiterin*, who has handled all the preparations and negotiated the details of the event with exemplary care.

This talk arises directly from my Balzan project "Literature as an object of knowledge". The project began in 2010 and ended officially in 2013, but still continues to flourish in various different "Balzan continuation projects", as we call them. I'd like to take this opportunity to say how much I owe to the enthusiasm and faithful collaboration of the whole Balzan project team, which comprised some twenty regular participants, most of them postdoctoral fellows and junior colleagues in different British universities. We also had a highly active senior advisory panel, and three of its members are here this evening. Professor Guillemette Bolens and Professor Michel Jeanneret, both from Geneva, are in the audience, and I'm very grateful to them for offering their support. I'm fortunate enough also to have the more visible and audible support of my colleague and friend Professor Elleke Boehmer, who has kindly agreed to act as respondent to my lecture, despite her extremely crowded life as a member of national and international committees: she has in fact rushed over here directly from an important meeting in London this morning.

Before the award ceremony in 2009, I was invited to deliver a short account of my research career at a seminar in the Swiss Academies in Berne, and today's lecture is in some sense a report on work completed and work still in progress. It expresses my personal view and methodology, but I believe that it also represents the core position of most project members.[1]

I shall begin by sketching out the general perspective within which the work of the project has taken shape over these last four or five years and consider some of the problems we have encountered, in particular the relation between literary study and cognitive science. The later part of the lecture will increasingly focus on literary texts.

THE SCOPE OF "LITERATURE"

For the purposes of the project, the word "literature" includes potentially all forms of story-telling, fiction-making, poetry, song, drama and their media equivalents. In other words, literature is regarded here as an ancient and fundamental human activity. This is in effect an anthropological use of the term, aimed at asking questions such as: What is literature for? Why do humans expend so much of their time and energy on these activities? More specifically: what is the value of literature as a vehicle and instrument of thought?

It hardly needs to be said that the way such activities and verbal artefacts are framed or conceptualized varies from culture to culture,

---

[1] Some of my remarks on cognition and cognitive science are taken (or developed) from my introduction to the special issue of *Paragraph* entitled "Reading Literature Cognitively", which I edited with Karin Kukkonen and Olivia Smith as a first collective publication from the project group. A more detailed account of the field as a whole can be found in my book *Thinking with Literature*, forthcoming from Oxford University Press.

both geographically and historically. The concept "literature" as it is widely used today arose in the eighteenth century from the earlier notion of "letters" (Latin *litterae*). It designates primarily a written mode of communication ("literacy") and a canon of works that are prized by a given culture. There is no other single word in English (or, as far as I know, in other European languages) that has that broader, more inclusive sense I mentioned a moment ago, and so I use it, as it were, by default.[2] However, I think that we should not be too nervous about using a value-laden term, provided that we are aware of its connotations. Evaluation is in fact fundamental to the way in which literary activities and artefacts (in the broader sense) are perceived. Assumptions such as "detective novels are not proper literature" are common in our own cultural and historical moment, and it seems likely that this way of attributing authenticity (and sometimes authority) to particular works is virtually universal, since evaluation is deeply embedded in human cognitive functioning. The various modes of literature are culturally *recognizable*, furthermore, as a special class of objects or activities: you are not likely to read a first-person novel as an autobiography unless the author is playing tricks on you (in which case the tricks themselves prove the point, since there cannot be tricks unless there is a set of orthodox responses). I should be surprised if this was not also the case, *mutatis mutandis*, in non-literate and pre-literate cultures.

The Object of Knowledge in Literary Studies

We turn now to literary studies as a discipline within the academy (and I refer here, of course, to the university institutions I am familiar with, those of "Western"[3] societies). The first question is: What is the object of knowledge in literary studies? Note that I am using the word "object" in two senses here: literature is the object of enquiry, but a literary object is a special kind of object or thing. Here are some obvious answers to our question:

---

[2] The distinction between fictional and non-fictional writing is also culturally variable; it becomes particularly problematic in cases such as religious or mythical narratives, which may be "fictional" for some, "non-fictional" for others, while the modern category "literature" includes both fictional and non-fictional modes of writing.

[3] I shall from now on use this word, and the word "literature" itself, without quotation marks, on the assumption that they will be understood to be crude approximations.

1. Unlike the objects studied in medicine (bodies, living tissues, disease) or in geology (solid material objects such as rocks), a literary work is a human artefact, and more specifically an object made of language.[4]
2. It is an object in history: an object shaped and modified by its trajectory through time, saturated in historical and cultural contexts; an object also of collective memory.
3. It is an aesthetic object, belonging to a broader class of objects that includes musical works, paintings, sculptures and other three-dimensional artworks.
4. Finally, literature is an object in social use: people buy, borrow, rent, download literary works of all kinds and "consume" them in a way that may sometimes seem obsessive.

This brings me to my next question, that of the relation between the academic study of literature and the public sphere.

Within the academic institutions of most Western cultures, the *study* of literature belongs to an interdisciplinary spectrum. In that spectrum, it shares common ground with linguistics, history, cultural studies, social studies, philosophy, psychology, anthropology (and others). It is, one might say, always a potentially interdisciplinary subject, and I shall return to that question shortly. However, it is important to point out first that literature is also an object of *public* attention, consumption and evaluation. In its various aspects – its fabrication, its delivery, its use – it is a familiar feature of the public domain. It does not require an institutionalized mode of analysis in order to achieve wide and effective use. So (people ask) how do we justify the academic study of literature? What is the academic study of literature for?

It is not difficult, I think, to agree on three main points:

1. Literary study deploys skills of historical investigation (research into texts and contexts). The public consumption of literature ultimately depends on those skills: people need reliable texts, and they seek knowledge about what they are reading.
2. It promotes the skills of attentive reading and understanding (interpretation) that are intrinsic to the experience of literature.
3. It offers the possibility of a sustained attempt to identify the literary object collectively, whether through poetics, aesthetics or more generally the many varieties of literary theory that have proliferated over the last fifty years or so.

---

[4] This remains the case even if one takes into account the mode of delivery (oral speech, a book made of paper, perhaps with illustrations, or a stream of electronic data), or if one includes visual media such as theatre or film.

The realization of these objectives is, however, far from straight-forward. I regard it as axiomatic that literary objects are highly specific: their value to those who use them resides in their particularity. They seem thus to require a particularized approach – what I have just referred to as the skills of attentive reading, commonly referred to as "close reading". The objective of theory, by contrast, is to generalize and universalize, and in the case of literature (as opposed to the study of human organs or geological strata) this gives rise to a certain tension with the object of study. A top-down relation between literary theory and critical practice will tend to suppress or at least divert the radical energies of individual literary works: it can result either in formal-istic modes of analysis or in conceptually programmatic varieties of inter-pretation. I want to insist that, if literary studies is to be something other than a branch of cultural history, of sociology or indeed of philo-sophy, it must always aim to respect – I repeat the phrase – the radical energies of individual literary works. Close reading cannot be by-passed or bracketed off.

On the other hand, as I have emphasized from the outset, the study of literature leads one to ask, from the bottom up, a broad range of questions about literature as a human activity. And that means that close reading cannot in itself suffice. It needs to be inserted into a wider interdisciplinary frame that is at once flexible and respectful of the spe-cial character of literature as an object of knowledge. So, when I was invited by the Balzan Foundation to design a project on which to spend their generous prize funding, I asked myself what kind of inter-disciplinary frame might meet those criteria.

The expanding galaxy of literary theories that characterized the late twentieth century had its own interdisciplinary connections: Saus-surean linguistics, psychoanalysis, structuralist anthropology, post-Marxist politics and sociology and post-phenomenological philosophy. I have drawn key insights throughout my career from that theoretical nexus, and I entirely respect the work of colleagues and institutions that are still pursuing those paths creatively in their own ways. But I believe that the time has come to take a fresh look at the whole field and think about where literary studies should go in the twenty-first century, and in particular where it might seek to place itself within the interdisciplinary ecology.

What I chose to focus on as the principal strand in the project was the possibility of a cognitive approach to the study of literature, and this is what we have been exploring in the last five years in a series of intensive workshops and discussion groups. I shall therefore now out-line that approach before looking at some specific literary texts within a cognitive frame.[5]

Towards a cognitive approach to literary study

We first need a working definition of "cognition". The word has often been used in philosophy and in everyday parlance to refer to rational thought and empirical perception as distinct from other mental processes, especially emotion and its grounding in the body. However, most cognitive scientists and many cognitive philosophers (in both the analytic and the phenomenological traditions) are now giving the word a much broader sense, embracing mental functioning and mental processes as a whole. These processes include not only abstract and rational thought but also imagination, emotion and sensorimotor reflexes and responses; they are assumed to be connected and mutually interactive. The biological mind, in other words, is not a computer; in the realm of cognitive science, thought is only imaginable nowadays as *embodied*, even if people continue to disagree about the conditions of its embodiment.

We can now ask why a cognitive approach to the study of litera-ture might be productive. A first answer is afforded by the existence and interest of what I call "the cognitive conversation". Cognition has in the last twenty-five years or so moved to the forefront of research in neuroscience, psychology, evolutionary anthropology, philosophy and linguistics. It is one of the most exciting and rapidly expanding fields of research, and is giving rise to interdisciplinary conversations across the whole spectrum from the physical sciences to the humanities. It is difficult to imagine that literary studies has nothing to gain from par-ticipating in those conversations. In addition, cognition and cognitive research are nowadays constantly in the news, and attract a great deal of public interest. It would be good for literary studies if we could

---

[5] Instead of providing references for specific points within my presentation, I have pre-ferred to append a selective list of references. It is meant simply as an indication of my own principal sources in preparing this lecture and as a preliminary guide for those who may be unfamiliar with the cognitive terrain.

draw on that source of public energy, not least because many of the forms of literary theory which have been practised in the last half-century are commonly regarded as esoteric, even wilfully so.

More specifically, literature is a mode of thought that exploits the full range of cognitive processes as I have described them: it takes for granted their interconnectedness, and thus maps extremely well onto the cognitive domain. It shows humans in their cognitive ecology, interacting with each other and with the world, and it probes the limits of the human capacity for imagining the world from alternative perspectives.

Finally, but also fundamentally, cognitive approaches offer a new perspective on the material out of which literature is made, that is to say language. That perspective is agent-driven and communicative rather than discourse-driven; it emphasizes the pragmatics of language use, its openness to improvisation rather than its subjection to conventions and codes; and it insists on the grounding of language in the body (human language is saturated with bodily inputs, in the first place because it is normally acquired situationally, in specific contexts; and secondly because of its own acoustic properties).

What, then, might a cognitive approach to literary study be capable of delivering? I would claim that it can potentially deliver *both* an intellectual and imaginative frame of reference within which to explore literature as a human activity, *and* a cognitive pragmatics for close reading. It would be imperative to demonstrate that these can work together, avoiding the "theory-practice" tension that I referred to earlier. I want indeed to emphasize here that the cognitive approach, as I envisage it, is not a theory, that is to say a single coherent set of arguments driven by a supposedly watertight logic. It derives its energies from an interdisciplinary context which in the current state of research has no common theoretical foundation. Nor should it be regarded as a new "turn" in existing literary theory – a "cognitive turn", following on from the linguistic turn, the historical turn, the cultural turn, the ethical turn and the like. It belongs not to the galaxy of late twentieth-century theories (although it might certainly be able to find points of viable connection with at least some of them) but to a different emerging set of preoccupations which at present has no single name, although the coining of the word "Anthropocene" to designate the current mutation in the planetary role and status of the human species is a sign that we are on the threshold of some such reconfiguration.

LITERATURE AND SCIENCE

Before moving on to detailed literary examples, I want to spend a few minutes commenting on the relation between literary studies and science that is implied by a cognitive approach. I am aware that some people in the humanities are resistant to the idea of a collaboration with the experimental sciences (especially neuroscience and experimental psychology), which seem alien to the spirit of study in our segment of the interdisciplinary spectrum. More specifically, they object to the fact that experimental science uses methodologies and protocols that are unproductive when applied to literature (its emphasis on quantification, measurability, falsifiability and the like); they claim – with some justification – that scientific discourse is reductive when used as a way of explaining cultural phenomena. They are dismissive about the idea that a feature of a complex literary work might be explained by the firing of a given set of neurons, or that tracking the eye-movements of readers might tell us something relevant to the activity of literary reading. Some protest also that a cognitive approach implies a rigorously phylogenetic set of assumptions which "essentialize" the brain, and thus the mind, on the basis of what is in fact a Western cultural perspective and even a Western ideological prejudice: to adopt such an approach would threaten the values and principles on which an ethical practice of cultural studies rests.

When these interdisciplinary misunderstandings arise, it often takes years to overcome them by means of patient dialogue, clarification of respective positions, familiarization with fundamental terminology, assumptions and methodological strategies. All I can do here is to offer, if not answers, then at least some possible ways forward:

1. Cognition – the way we think – is arguably the most fundamentally *human* phenomenon one can choose to investigate; it can therefore only be properly investigated in a cross-disciplinary context where both the sciences and the humanities cooperate on something approaching equal terms.
2. The aim, for those of us in the humanities, is not to acquire at second hand a hard-core empirical knowledge for which we simply find "examples" in literature. Our corpus is already, in its constitution, a cognitive corpus: as I have already suggested, it is an embodiment of how humans think, how they have thought the world and themselves at different times and in different places. Scientists, in my experience, are extremely interested in hearing what we, as specialists, have to say about it.

3. Human cognition is not a static inherited brain structure. It is expressed through its signature products, language and culture. Culture is not antithetical to nature; it is a product of nature and a specialized extension of it. Another way of putting this is to say that the evolutionary niche exploited by the human brain is cognitive fluidity, improvisation, imagination: these give rise to *cultural* evolution.

4. Scientific research draws on precisely these capacities or skills: it depends on counterfactual thinking, imagining what does not (yet) exist, or a possibility not yet proven. And these of course are the skills that drive both the creation and the study of literature.

Here is one microscopic example of that last point. Among the fragments of Rebecca Elson's never-completed poem "Explaining Dark Matter", the following line stands out: "As if, from fireflies, one could infer the field."[6] Rebecca Elson was a research astrophysicist who was also a poet. She died in 1999 at the age of 39, leaving some notebooks full of verse and prose fragments in addition to a significant body of completed poems. Many of those poems are on scientific themes; one is called "Explaining Relativity", and it is clear that the idea of providing a poetic analogy for the hypothetical existence of dark matter preoccupied her a great deal.

Dark matter (which is, as I understand it, in part at least an energy field) is in effect invisible: one can only infer its presence from the behaviour of the luminous bodies in the cosmos. Hence Elson's analogy: in the darkness, you might infer the existence of the field from the visible fireflies.[7] Scientists of all kinds, including cognitive scientists, have to work inferentially: human cognition has direct access only to a very narrow spectrum of information about the physical world and indeed about ourselves. One of the key functions of cognition is to filter that limited and fragmentary stream of information, pick out what is salient or likely to be important for us, and enrich it, give it a meaning which is relevant to us.

----

[6] REBECCA ELSON, *A Responsibility to Awe*, p. 71. This fragment is dated July 1992. Elson returned to this theme (but without the fireflies) in October 1993 (p. 86) and June 1996 (pp. 107-108).

[7] The ironic or dismissive sense of "As if..." ("As if he thought I could fly the plane myself!") is excluded here, since it would disqualify the analogy. However, Elson is clearly evoking something like a counterfactual: the presence of fireflies is by no means certain evidence of the existence of a field. In other words, she seems to want to highlight the strangeness of the scientific deduction.

Elson is speaking about exactly that procedure in this fragmentary line. She clearly understood it very well, not only as a scientist, but also as a poet. It has a double aspect: underspecification, whether of the phenomena we perceive, or of the language we use in communicating with one another, and the inferential processes that underspecification triggers. That conjunction is central to the cognitive perspective on literature: it addresses the question of how readers and audiences supply the materials towards which a poem or a fictional storyworld gestures, the way it offers to our imagination an invisible field. So we arrive here at the very centre of the question of the literary imagination, which is one variant of the human ability to imagine the non-existent or the not yet existent. This explains why I chose as my title quotation: "Far other worlds, and other seas".

I shall be coming in a moment to the poem from which that line is taken, but first I want to introduce some of the principal analytical instruments of cognitive literary study, using another short quotation.

"BOOKS ARE NOT ABSOLUTELY DEAD THINGS"

The quotation is taken this time from Milton's *Areopagitica* of 1644, one of the most eloquent arguments against censorship ever written:

> Books are not absolutely dead things, but do contain a potency of life in them to be as active as that soul was whose progeny they are; nay they do preserve as in a vial[8] the purest efficacy and extraction of that living intellect that bred them.[9]

Let's paraphrase Milton's famous remark, adjusting it a little to suit the perspective of someone interested in the value and function of literature in a cognitive perspective.

1. Literature is clearly, by definition, a product of human cognition (the mind or "soul" in Milton's language),[10] reflecting, as I said earlier, the full com-

---

[8] A small glass bottle containing precious fluids such as drugs, medicines, etc.

[9] JOHN MILTON, *Complete Prose Works*, vol. 2, p. 492. I have modernized the spelling.

[10] The word "soul" in Milton's day could refer either to the supernatural entity that survives death according to Christian belief, or to the agent of human action in the world, i.e., what we would call "the mind".

plexity and mobility of cognition, and acting also as a kind of archive of cognitive possibilities.

2. As an instrument of human cognition, literature is continuous with spoken language (it has a primary communicative function), yet with a longer life-span than everyday communication (it is "preserved", as Milton puts it, whether by memory, writing or print), and it is more sustainedly and concentratedly reflective.

3. The agency of individual human thought acting through this instrument that it has invented has a peculiar power: we recognize it as the product of a living creature. Perceiving the intended movement or action of another living being is exactly what makes one see that it *is* a living being in the first place.

4. The old analogy between books and offspring ("my book is my baby") as reformulated by Milton still delivers the intuition of deep biological relation between thought and the body that makes it much more than a metaphor.

One strand is especially dominant in this complex bundle: the recognition of life, the living, relies on the assumption of agency. This insight can be explored in a number of different directions.

First, it justifies the reading of literature not as neutral text but as a living instrument of extended cognition;[11] it is one of the principal tools we use in order to challenge the constraints of immediate real-world experience and reach out into alternative ways of configuring the world and our perceptions of it.

Secondly, it justifies the whole set of critical moves that are opened up by the notion of kinesis: the instinctive recognition of embodied life and intention that is communicated by bodily posture and gesture. Here is a brief example. Imagine yourself walking through a crowded pedestrian precinct, with people coming at you from all angles, dogs, small children, older people with sticks, a cyclist weaving her way through, teenagers engrossed in their mobiles and not looking where they are going. You avoid bumping into them, automatically making rapid calculations of their speed and trajectory in relation to your own, sometimes making brief eye contact. All these passers-by offer themselves to be read as individuals with particular postures, habits of being, but you almost instantly discard those possible readings. Now think about what would happen if you saw someone emerge from the crowd with a posture like this:

---

[11] Other variants of this expression currently in use include "extended mind" and perhaps especially "distributed cognition".

> He was an inch, perhaps two, under six feet, powerfully built, and he ad-
> vanced straight at you with a slight stoop of the shoulders, head forward, and
> a fixed-from-under stare which made you think of a charging bull.[12]

This individual catches your attention, becomes salient for you. You begin to interpret the posture as a psychological as well as a physical habit; you begin to draw inferences about the life-story that it implies.

This is the opening sentence of Joseph Conrad's novel *Lord Jim* (1900). It is a highly kinesic sentence, focusing on a stoop and a stare: a posture that begins already to trigger the process of cognitive reading that will unfold throughout the novel, broadening to a global level as it proceeds. I shall be saying more about that later, but for now I want to use the example as a bridge to a further point arising from Milton's insight.

Kinesis and the agency that it implies lead one – imperfectly, un-reliably, but irresistibly – into the labyrinth of other people's minds, their beliefs, their feelings, their intentions, their promises and their deceits, since we cannot perceive others as being alive unless we can imagine that they have thought-worlds. "Mind-reading" (or "theory of mind", the attribution of mind-states) is a central topic in various kinds of cognitive psychology and in evolutionary studies of human cognition. It emerged into the limelight in cognitive research some 25 years ago in connection with studies of autism, and it leads directly into the question of empathy, which is a major concern in the understanding of imaginative writing of all kinds.[13]

We can now take these cognitive terms and principles further through a reading of more extended literary examples. From now on, the energies of these texts will provide the momentum: in other words, their function is not simply to "illustrate" a point from cognitive science.

---

[12] JOSEPH CONRAD, *Lord Jim*, p. 3.

[13] It is important to point out, however, that empathy, however defined, is not synonymous with mind-reading. One can attempt to understand other people's mental processes without feeling empathy, as when a detective or a historian attempts to grasp the motives of a particular agent. Mind-reading is also required, arguably, in order to understand any communicative act.

A GREEN THOUGHT IN A GREEN SHADE

My title quotation is taken from Andrew Marvell's "The Garden" (ca. 1668). It is a poem consisting of nine stanzas; these are the fifth and the sixth:

> What wondrous life is this I lead!
> Ripe apples drop about my head;
> The luscious clusters of the vine
> Upon my mouth do crush their wine;
> The nectarene, and curious peach
> Into my hands themselves do reach;
> Stumbling on melons, as I pass,
> Insnared with flow'rs, I fall on grass.
>
> Meanwhile the mind, from pleasures less,
> Withdraws into its happiness:
> The mind, that ocean where each kind
> Does straight its own resemblance find;
> Yet it creates, transcending these,
> Far other worlds, and other seas;
> Annihilating all that's made
> To a green thought in a green shade.[14]

These two stanzas form a brilliant diptych representing the modes of body and mind: it would be hard in fact to find a more imaginatively persuasive articulation of embodied cognition in poetic form.

I want first to pick out some salient features of stanza 1. This is emphatically not a *description* of a garden: it stages an almost erotically intimate interaction of speaker and environment. That staging relies heavily on the use of kinesic verbs (dropping, crushing, stumbling). One of the ways that Marvell induces these kinesic responses is by the inversion of subject and object. The garden and its fruits become the subject of kinesic verbs: the fruit, not the hands, are doing the dropping, crushing and reaching. Even where the speaker is the subject, in the last two lines, the fruit and flowers remain the agents: in the early modern period, the word "curious" had a range of meanings, which in this case clearly include "delicate", "exquisite", but it already had

---

[14] NIGEL SMITH (ed.), *The Poems of Andrew Marvell*, pp. 157-158. For the poem as a whole, together with detailed commentary and notes, see pp. 152-159 in this edition.

the sense "inquisitive", which makes the peach an anthropomorphic agent, inquisitively reaching out to the human presence in the garden. In consequence, the speaker is represented as not only engaged with, but absorbed into the vegetable world of the garden, as if he were simply part of the natural ecology. This is what in cognitive terms would be called an enactive representation.

We turn now to stanza 2. Commentators have helpfully explained lines 3-4 of this stanza as referring to an idea which was already beginning to be outdated when Marvell wrote the poem: the idea that for every land creature, there is an analogous sea creature. It does not matter whether Marvell himself believed it, or whether *we* believe it: it is a metaphor for the way the mind works. These lines and the two lines that follow are about thinking, cognition: the way the human mind represents the world, both as it is and as it might be.

The notion of mental representation is the subject of endless controversy, both in cognitive psychology and in literary studies. We do not need to engage with that debate here: the fact is that our perceptual and cognitive systems deliver functional equivalents of the perceived world. I can walk through a garden, eating ripe fruit and stumbling on melons, and I can then sit down in the shade, perhaps with my eyes shut, and "imagine" the garden, call up functionally valid representations of it, or indeed of other things; if I have the skills of an Andrew Marvell, I can write a poem about it. Thanks to its embodied nature, language enables such representations to be transmitted to others, again in functionally valid ways. So Marvell's brief account of the way the mind represents the world is far from naive. It even alludes to the characteristic rapidity of cognitive representations that makes them so difficult to grasp as processes ("straight" means "straight away", "immediately").

This is, however, only step one of the withdrawal into the mind. Step two is elegantly indicated in lines 5-6. Representing the world to enable you to engage in it enactively is what all creatures with evolved neurological systems do. Representing it freely when it is *not* present to you (metarepresentation) is something quite different, and it seems in fact that this is the defining difference between animal and human cognition. As I said earlier, humans have prospered in evolutionary terms primarily because they have acquired cognitive fluidity: the ability to improvise, imagine alternatives, plan for the future and also recall episodes from the past (episodic memory). They can devise thought experiments; they can construct hypotheses and conjectures; and they can of course also invent fictional storyworlds and poetic imagery. This is what Marvell is talking about here. But it's crucial to notice that he's not only thinking of his own poetic creativity in devising this paradise garden of his own. Imagination is an everyday resource that we draw on, for example, every time we use conditional constructions ("If I were you, I'd take that job"). One of the prime attractions of the cognitive approach is that it connects the literary with the everyday. To paraphrase Marvell's parallel between land creatures and sea creatures: there is nothing in the world of the imagination that does not have a counterpart in the everyday world.

Now to the last two lines of the extract. The phrase "Annihilating all that's made" is a hyperbolic way of evoking the human capacity for conceptualization, our key cognitive tool (along with language itself). The human species has thrived on the skill of replacing the bewildering plurality of particular things in the world with categories and concepts. Thus a green thought is a quintessentialization of the garden – its greenness, which absorbs as it were all its other aspects. But note that this "green thought" is still a sensual or somatic imagination, and it takes place within a real garden: it is produced by the garden. The poem is not a eulogy of abstraction: it proposes a reciprocal interchange between body and mind, thought and the world.

THE POSTURE OF READING

I chose the Marvell example because it so graphically displays a cluster of cognitive themes, together with some of the moves that would be made by a cognitively inflected criticism. I turn finally to a short passage from Conrad's *Lord Jim*, and here the point is to show at least schematically how you can link that style of criticism to questions with the broadest ethical and cultural reach.

The passage can be understood even if you have not read the novel. All you need to know is that a group of listeners gather in this scene to hear the fictional character Marlow tell a story. The story is about a young English naval officer who, under pressure, makes a disastrous error of judgement which is also a transgression against British codes of honour.

Perhaps it would be after dinner, on a veranda draped in motionless foliage and crowned with flowers, in the deep dusk speckled by fiery cigar-ends. The elongated bulk of each cane-chair harboured a silent listener. Now and then a small red glow would move abruptly, and expanding light up the fingers of a languid hand, part of a face in profound repose, or flash a crimson gleam into a pair of pensive eyes overshadowed by a fragment of an unruffled forehead; and with the very first word uttered Marlow's body, extended at rest in the seat, would become very still, as though his spirit had winged its way back into the lapse of time and were speaking through his lips from the past.[15]

For Conrad's novels, the phrase "far other worlds, and other seas" can be read literally as well as metaphorically. The verandah where the listeners hear Marlow tell Jim's story opens out onto a global perspective, crossed and criss-crossed by voyages between Europe, Africa and Asia; in that sense one might even think of it as an immensely expanded version of Marvell sitting in his green thought-world imagining the abundant world of the garden. The novel, like the poem, imagines a cognitive vantage-point for reflection.

The community of listeners is culturally specific. One of its coordinates is the all-male world of the navy; but there is also a global perspective focusing on issues of ethnicity – the listeners are white Europeans in a colonial setting, and a key leitmotif of the novel is the phrase "he was one of us". However, it is essential to note the "Perhaps" at the beginning of this passage, which affords a perspective onto an endless series of other possible audiences – non-European ones for example, or audiences that include women.[16]

This possibility is enhanced by the fact that, in this scene, the listeners do not appear as individual figures: their faces are in shadow, with fleeting glimpses of eyes and facial expressions – the scene is highly underspecified (one is reminded of Rebecca Elson's fireflies and of the inferences they afford). The listeners emerge from the darkness above all as shapes within chairs – as *postures*. Their posture, which is shared by the story-teller, is both relaxed and focused. The scene is very like a theatre: the listeners sit expectantly in the dark, ready to engage in a communal act of focused attention and reflective cognition.

---

[15] CONRAD, *Lord Jim*, pp. 24-25.

[16] It may be helpful here to supply the sentence that precedes the quoted passage: "And later on, many times, in distant parts of the world, Marlow showed himself willing to remember Jim, to remember him at length, in detail and audibly" (p. 24).

What they are focusing on here is a difficult human case: a problem of agency (how much is intentional, how much is pre-reflective action prompted by pressure of circumstances), and therefore a problem of ethics. They will require considerable resources of empathy in order to avoid prejudging the case. They will need to conduct an inferential calculus of mind-reading: what may be presumed to have gone on in Jim's mind, both during the disastrous event itself and in its aftermath; and they will have to think beyond the horizon of their own ethnic and cultural formation – to interrogate everything that is implied by the phrase "he was one of us". All this is already anticipated by the opening sentence of the novel quoted above: an initial cognitive response opens out onto the whole enquiry into a particular life and its ethical and ethnic implicatures.

There are many directions in which such readings might be taken,[17] but I want to suggest that they might provide the foundation for an argument against the habit of over-conceptualization, or over-hasty conceptualization, that has characterized a good deal of literary interpretation. Literature, as I said earlier, makes us read from the bottom up. There are so many modes of academic discourse that insist on a top-down approach that it can be hard to listen to the way literature thinks. Listening to the way literature thinks is in essence what I believe literary study should teach us to do.

What I have been talking about today, then, is literature as an object of knowledge, but with a more specific angle: literature as a way of thinking. Literature invites study as an object of knowledge because of its complexity, its resistance to codification, its resourcefulness, but also its accessibility. It demands a special and extended use of the cognitive resources that we use daily, in particular a heightened attentiveness (so this is about the process of reading, listening to, understanding literature). It therefore lends itself to cognitively inflected study, analysis, criticism (so this is about the methodology, the use of new or updated explanatory frames of reference and instruments of analysis). Since literature is an arena in which cognitive processes are made visible without being turned into pure concepts or measurable items, it also becomes a valid source of potential insights for cognitive science.

---

[17] For a detailed and contextualized reading of the Conrad passage, see the chapter "The Posture of Reading: Joseph Conrad's *Lord Jim*" in my forthcoming book *Thinking with Literature*.

Rather than being a passive receiver of paradigms from elsewhere, literary study thus has the opportunity at this moment in cultural evolution to present a challenge not only to its own practitioners, but also to colleagues in philosophy, psychology and the physical sciences, to think outside the logical or quantifiable box. It offers to take us back to the way we actually think: a mode of thought that is embodied, imaginatively expansive and flexible.

EPILOGUE

So I shall end, not with those general remarks, but with an individual testimony to literature as an embodiment of reflection. The last fragment in Rebecca Elson's notebook, dated Monday 3 May 1999, palpably echoes Marvell's "The Garden":[18]

> In the garden of greens and shade
> Of a May fresh from April
> One foot already in June,
> Impatient to explore each last possibility
> Of green from the blue lavender,
> To the quintessential cherry
> To the yellowing, drying fritillaries
> Whose day came back in March.
> Impatient to say all these greens
> Before the flowers begin to chatter,
> To become loud with colour,
> To let themselves go lewdly and loudly
> Into scarlet, purples and indigos.

I include this poem, incomplete and half-formed as it is, because it is like a message in a bottle (a "vial", as Milton would have said), sent out to all of us by someone who knew she would never come home. On a particular day and a particular date, marked for us now by the death that came less than two weeks later, the astrophysicist Rebecca Elson recorded a moment of special intensity in a garden. In order to do that, she recrafted the message of the earlier poet, no longer young but not conscious of imminent extinction, who had recorded his par-

---

[18] ELSON, *A Responsibility to Awe*, p. 145.

ticular moment in a garden, his green thought in a green shade. She did it with a different cognitive instrument, namely her knowledge of the colour spectrum, but from her vantage point in a garden ecology, she signalled both backwards and forwards in time, enriching the possibilities of reflection on the living and the dead.

As you see, books – and especially perhaps those strangely powerful instruments of thought that we call poems – are not absolutely dead things.

SELECTED REFERENCES

BARSALOU, LAWRENCE W. "Situated Simulation in the Human Conceptual System." *Language and Cognitive Processes* 18 (2003): 513-562.

BOLENS, GUILLEMETTE. *Le Style des Gestes: Corporéité et kinésie dans le récit littéraire*. Lausanne: Éditions BHMS, 2008; English version: *The Style of Gestures: Embodiment and Cognition in Literary Narrative*. Baltimore: The Johns Hopkins University Press, 2012.

CARSTON, ROBYN. *Thoughts and Utterances: The Pragmatics of Explicit Communication*. Oxford: Blackwell, 2002.

CAVE, TERENCE. *Thinking with Literature: Towards a Cognitively Inflected Criticism*. Oxford: Oxford University Press, forthcoming 2015-16.

CAVE, TERENCE, KARIN KUKKONEN and OLIVIA SMITH, eds. *Reading Literature Cognitively*. Special edition of *Paragraph* 37 (2014).

CONRAD, JOSEPH. *Lord Jim*. Edited by Jacques Berthoud. Oxford World's Classics. Oxford: Oxford University Press, 2002.

COSMIDES, LEDA and JOHN TOOBEY. "Consider the Source: The Evolution of Adaptations for Decoupling and Metarepresentations." In *Metarepresentations: A Multidisciplinary Perspective*, edited by Dan Sperber, 53-111. Oxford: Oxford University Press, 2000.

CURRIE, GREGORY. *Arts and Minds*. Oxford: Oxford University Press, 2004.

ELSON, REBECCA. *A Responsibility to Awe*. Manchester: Carcanet Press, 2001.

FRITH, CHRISTOPHER D. *Making Up the Mind: How the Brain Creates Our Mental World*. Oxford: Blackwell, 2007.

GLENBERG, ARTHUR M. and MICHAEL P. KASCHAK. "Grounding Language in Action." *Psychonomic Bulletin and Review* 9 (2002): 558-565.

HARRIS, PAUL. *The Work of the Imagination*. Oxford: Blackwell, 2000.

KAHNEMAN, DANIEL. *Thinking, Fast and Slow*. London: Penguin Books, 2011.

MARVELL, ANDREW, see SMITH, NIGEL, ed.

MILTON, JOHN. *Complete Prose Works*. Edited by Ernest Sirluck. Vol. 2. New Haven: Yale University Press, 1959.

SCHAEFFER, JEAN-MARIE. *Pourquoi la fiction?* Paris: Seuil, 1999; English version *Why Fiction?* Translated by Dorrit Cohn. Lincoln: University of Nebraska Press, 2010.

SMITH, NIGEL, ed. *The Poems of Andrew Marvell*, revised ed. London and New York: Routledge, 2013.

SPERBER, DAN and DEIRDRE WILSON. *Relevance: Communication and Cognition*. Oxford: Blackwell, 1995; 1st ed. 1986.

TURNER, MARK. *The Literary Mind*. Oxford: Oxford University Press, 1996.

WALTON, KENDALL L. *Mimesis as Make-Believe: On the Foundations of the Representational Arts*. Cambridge, MA and London: Harvard University Press, 1990.

WHITEN, ANDREW, ROBERT A. HINDE, CHRISTOPHER B. STRINGER and KEVIN N. LALAND. *Culture Evolves*. Oxford: Oxford University Press, 2011.

ZUNSHINE, LISA. *Why We Read Fiction: Theory of Mind and the Novel*. Columbus: The Ohio State University Press, 2006.

COMMENT BY ELLEKE BOEHMER

Professor of World Literature in English, University of Oxford

Good evening, everyone. It's a great pleasure to be here to give this response at the University of Berne to Professor Terence Cave. Thank you to the very efficient team who brought me here, eventually at something of a trot, because I did indeed have the meeting to attend this morning in London that Terence described. But everything worked out very well, thanks to your excellent planning, and here I am.

It's also a great honour to speak in response to Terence Cave's Balzan lecture, in a curious way a well-timed honour. The organizers may not have known that Terence and I are long-term friends and on the 7th of October this year, just ten days ago, it struck me recently, had known each other for exactly twenty-nine years. So it was as a long-standing friend, but also as a curious writer, reader and critic, that, more recently, I have got so much pleasure from participating in many of the Balzan workshops and activities, even while acting as that slightly recalcitrant person who tended to ask the tricky questions, usually right at the end of the seminar, about cultural difference. Perhaps that was one of the reasons I was invited here this afternoon, to continue asking questions, and to think carefully about some of the intriguing but not always self-evident new ways into literature that Terence's work is positing. These new ways certainly represent an area that I'm going to respond to tonight, and this intellectual pleasure, added to the social one, makes it the more a joy to be here.

I have named my response, hopefully not too grandiosely, 'Other seas again, thinking with literature in the world.' The persuasive force of Professor Terence Cave's lectures, as we have experienced it here, rises from his ability to shine a clear, fresh light into the complicated devices through which literary structures work, and through which our thought is given shape, and make them seem completely self-evident, as if we had known how they do what they do all along.

Of course, as readers we do know about that **how**, through our practice, but we do so in the main intuitively. The beauty of Terence Cave's work on literature as a mode of thought is that he allows us at one and the same time to immerse ourselves in the writing, *and* to step back from it and to observe how those intuitions work: how literature helps us think our way through the world; what its inner linguistic operations are. It is a great honour to respond to him today.

Professor Cave's lecture has given us a characteristically generous overview of literature as a means through which thought is given embodied form. In my short response I propose to take a more minimalist or micro-view, looking at just three examples of how literary devices work cognitively. I want to put into focussed play the different kinds of attention that Terence's way of reading makes possible: first, in a brief kinesic or kinaesthetic reading of my own, to evoke how productive I find this approach; and then in two cases in relation to my own field, that of postcolonial or world literature in English.

This is, interestingly, not a field that has to date been much explored from a cognitive perspective. Till quite recently, postcolonial readings have been to an extent circumscribed by an attention – a rightful attention in political and ethical terms – to cultural difference, to the attempt to assert a distance through modes of representation from what is called the mind of Europe, as Dipesh Chakrabarty terms it in *Provincializing Europe*.

Yet this very different writing from many of Terence Cave's examples provides, I feel, an interesting potential limit case to the effectiveness of the mode of cognitive reading he has demonstrated for us. It is one that I feel ultimately collapses that limit and so widens the field of possibility for this kind of reading. In my response, I am therefore taking the cognitive pragmatics that Terence has explored with us and showing how richly the approach can also be adapted in non-European literary fields. I am not, however, implying that a universal mind is thereby at work, or that these fields are somehow being attached to Europe in a merely affiliative and derivative way. What is at work in all of these cases is the human activity of literature, that is, the literary work of making verbal form, rhythm and story, which is work that happens across cultures. It is for this reason that I have drawn together examples from Europe, Asia and the Caribbean. Literature as a mode of imaginative thinking matters in all the different traditions emerging from these spaces.

1. KINESIC READING

The richness of approach Terence has explored with us is persuasively exemplified in *kinesic reading*. With this term I refer to that way in which our interaction with a piece of literature is not merely static and silent but involves or invokes gesture and other movement in the very act of reading, reception and interpretation. This is common to all cultures in some shape or form, not least to oral cultures. Consider how refrain works in participatory songs and poems, such as nursery rhymes, rounds, or clapping songs.

To help us think more closely about this particular mode of reception, I take as an evocative instance the following short extract from a poem that is a particular favourite of mine, "The Rime of the Ancient Mariner" by Samuel Taylor Coleridge. The stanza, which is a classic ballad stanza rhyming *abcb*, recounts that torrid time when the mariner's ship is becalmed, and he alone on board remains alive, all the other sailors have been struck down by a mysterious curse. I feel it is especially appropriate to bring in here as the tale the Mariner tells has a trans-oceanic and global dimension. And like Terence Cave's example from Marvell, this poem, too, talks about 'far other worlds'. In the quotation, I would like in particular to draw attention to the second, highlighted line:

> Alone, alone, all, all alone,
> **Alone on a wide wide sea!**
> And never a saint took pity on
> My soul in agony.
> (Samuel Taylor Coleridge, 'The Rime of the Ancient Mariner', Part IV, stanza iii)

In a traditional close reading we might have said that the repetition in the highlighted line was for emphasis. The expanse of the sea is brought across to us through how both the sound and the semantics of the repetition of 'wide' invites us to dwell on the idea of width. But now notice how we interact with the line somatically, as we read it. How the repetition moves the mouth. The 'wah' sounds stretch the mouth wide, horizontally, emphasizing or re-emphasizing breadth, amplitude; the horizon when at sea. The open sound and the repetition almost invites a stretch open of the arms, a reaching out to that extensive horizon. And then there is the recursive effect that comes with the repetition. Notice how we are taken back by the second 'wide' to ponder on the idea of that blank cursed sea: of its desert-like expanse, with not a drop to drink; of its absence of humanity. Against this broad, blank background, the solitude of the Mariner is sharply accentuated. Moreover, both the aural and the semantic qualities of 'all, all alone' are deeper kinesic resonance in 'wide wide sea'. As readers we feel ourselves, as is the Mariner, confronted by that wide expanse of water, and dwarfed by it in our singleness.

Now I move on to the two examples from my own field of work, or postcolonial literature in English.

Something I found very valuable in Terence Cave's talk, when he referred to literature as a human activity, was his sensitive avoidance of the implication that some universal mind is at work when we ascribe certain affordances to literary texts. Thereby he also side-stepped the condescension that metropolitan interpretative approaches have sometimes expressed *vis à vis* material from outside Europe. Terence achieved this by showing us how specificity matters – a specificity of language, of form; how literary shape or structure in and of itself matters. Importantly, this assumption pertains whatever literature we are looking at. The approach does not privilege one kind of writing, say, the epic, over another; or one kind of literary tradition over another. All these operations are in play wherever language is used to make art, to make literature.

In respect of postcolonial writing and criticism, therefore, the approach Terence Cave has offered us allows us to consider how literary form is as important as 'content' in reading and understanding postcolonial literature. This is an important intervention in a field that is in the main historically and politically defined, where writing is valued first and foremost for its 'message' (be it liberation or resistance), and criticism privileges instrumentality, giving relatively little regard to how the texts concerned put that message across or encode postcolonial knowledge. I believe that insights from cognitive reading help us to address this neglect in the field. They help us to consider how postcolonial fiction and poetry structurally embed certain forms of postcolonial awareness. And this then allows us to ask some radical questions. Can literary texts be read as formally postcolonial? Are there particular features which allow us to speak of certain kinds of writing as clarifying of or giving insights into postcolonial conditions? I would say there are, but in claiming this, I do not also claim that these effects are unique to this field. On the contrary, they have been observed and described across many other literary critical domains, but have been left relatively under-discussed in this one.

To demonstrate the power of cognitive approaches in my field, I will offer just two examples.

2. NAVIGATING SPACE IN TEXT

In my work I am particularly interested in how literature conceives of, maps and reflects space. These are all important tasks in situations where certain spaces (public spaces, city streets, enclosed squares and gardens) are not equally available to all, or on the same terms to all. Postcolonial writing of the city – the work of Ivan Vladislavić, Katherine Boo, Brian Chikwava, and a host of others – arguably allows the reader imaginative access to such forbidden or restricted spaces and the effect is, potentially at least, liberatory. Kinesics comes into this, in so far as the writing will through its imaginative and formal capacities navigate through these spaces, 'building' and 'opening up' the city as it moves and progresses.

> 'pedestrians, rickshaws, scooters, taxis, buses, and cows pick[ing] their way around each other.'

> '[Nisha's] new home was above her husband's shop. Its entrance was from the back gully, a dumping place for rubbish. The paving was rutted and uneven, the foot slipped between the debris of eternal construction, loose brick, piles of sand, bajri, and puddles of stagnant water.'

> Manju Kapur, *Home*, pp. 109-110; 322.

In my two examples from the Delhi writer Manju Kapur's novel *Home*, notice how the copious, pile-up lists that she uses, kinesically, as it were, pick their way through the crowded city streets. Recurring right the way across *Home*, these lists littered with commas and piled-up adjectives, give the impression of a city that, in the words of commentator Rana Dasgupta, is 'hyper-accelerated', at one and the same time 'already mature' and decaying; anarchic and yet hypermodern (*Capital*, p. 439). The piled-up effects allow readers to try to make imaginative sense of the city in all its impossible, well-nigh inconceivable fullness and chaos.

3. Re-imagining colonial history

My final example is drawn from a much anthologized poem by the Saint Lucian poet and Nobel prizewinner Derek Walcott. "Ruins of a Great House" is a haunting and haunted poem, a contradictory indictment-in-elegy-form of New World slavery. In the poem, the speaker, himself a descendant of slaves, revisits a former slave plantation and meditates on the history and the aftermath of this ruinous form of human trafficking.

As with my other examples, the language is rich with complex and resonant imagery, to which I unfortunately do not have time to do justice. But by way of rounding off this short response, I would like to draw our attention to Walcott's use of repetition, in several recursive loops, in particular of green imagery, and of references to the English literary tradition, which keeps taking us back to the conflicting loyalties and passions that possess the speaker. The poet at one and the same time links back to, disavows and yet also embraces that same green English world of Andrew Marvell, and the world of the early seventeenth century, which has spawned the literature he loves. I have tried to point to these significant, and in part kinesic, repetitions using highlighting:

Stones only, the ***disjecta membra*** of this Great House,
Whose moth-like girls are mixed with candledust,
Remain to file the lizard's dragonish claws;
The mouths of those gate cherubs streaked with stain.
Axle and coachwheel silted under the muck
Of cattle droppings.
                    Three crows flap for the trees,
And settle, creaking the eucalyptus boughs.
A smell of dead limes quickens in the nose
The leprosy of Empire.

'Farewell, green fields'
'Farewell, ye happy groves'

A green lawn, broken by low walls of stone
Dipped to a rivulet, and pacing, I thought next
Of men like **Hawkins, Walter Raleigh, Drake**,
Ancestral murderers and poets, more perplexed
In memory now by every ulcerous crime.
The world's green age then was a rotting lime
Whose stench became the charnel galleon's text.

The rot remains with us, the men are gone.
But, as dead ash is lifted in a wind,
That fans the blackening ember of the mind,
My eyes burned from the ashen prose of **Donne**.
Ablaze with rage, I thought
Some slave is rotting in this manorial lake,
And still the coal of my compassion fought:
That Albion too, was once
A colony like ours, 'Part of the continent, piece of the main'
Nook-shotten, rook o'er blown, deranged
By foaming channels, and the vain expense
Of bitter faction.
All in compassion ends
So differently from what the heart arranged:
'as well as if a manor of thy friend's...'
Derek Walcott, 'Ruins of a Great House', *In a Green Night*, pp. 9-10.

   As the poet attempts to make sense of his painful history, his island story of ruination, his mind moves through a series of fragments: we see him flitting between different points of literary reference, including quotations from Thomas Browne and John Donne. The poem holds two countervailing processes in tension, the breaking apart of Walcott's thinking and remembering under the pressure of his anger, and his passionate interest in bringing these different fragments together, to see what might be salvaged from history. We sense both processes at work, and the shape and movement of the poem dramatizes the tension between them, the green links to Albion and Keats, yet also to rot and decay. His thought gains form, sustenance, and hope from the salvage activity. A cycle has ended, and rightly so. A poem of new allegiance, of reconciled belonging is created from what remains. The reader moves together with the poet as he stumbles determinedly across these fragments, as if clambering over stones, just as we moved together with the dynamic tracking and mapping sentences of Coleridge and of Kapur, earlier, as well as of Marvell and of Conrad, in Terence's reading.

   Without making too great a claim for one reading over others, what I hope I have demonstrated here in brief, in response to Terence's *ars critica*, or even *ars poetica*, is how we can follow literary cognitive processes at work in different times and cultures. In doing so, we make no distinction between one time or place over another. Rather, we feel encouraged to marvel anew at the variousness and ingenuity of the human mind – on and through different seas and in other worlds.

REFERENCES

CHAKRABARTY, DIPESH. *Provincializing Europe: Postcolonial Thought and Historical Difference*. Princeton: Princeton University Press, 2000.

DASGUPTA, RANA. *Capital*. London: Granta, 2014.

KAPUR, MANJU. *Home*. London: Faber, 2006.

WALCOTT, DEREK. *In a Green Night*. London: Cape, 1962.

DISCUSSION AND QUESTIONS

Thomas Claviez: Both Professor Cave's talk and Professor Boehmer's response opened indeed other worlds and other seas, and we might like to explore these. The floor is open for questions.

First question from the audience: A lot of what you've said has to do with embodiment, if I understood you right. Now, if I try to translate 'embodiment' in French, I get 'incarnation', and it doesn't really mean the same thing, does it?

Terence Cave: No, it doesn't.

First question from the audience: So my question is: how much of what you've done is related to your Anglo-Saxon culture? Would a French guy have come to the same developments, or would Montaigne have invented the same way of looking at literature as you have?

Terence Cave: Thank you for that very pertinent question. In general, I think it's true that people live in different cultural thought-worlds and language worlds, but those differences are always negotiable, provided that there are enough common reference points. Montaigne's thought-world belongs to the prehistory of modern cognitive science, but he would no doubt have found it hard to come to terms with the scientific revolution and its technologies. As for 'embodiment', that's a good example of the kind of vocabulary which is difficult to translate before a parallel scientific culture has developed in the target language. This happens all the time, in European law and politics, in the physical sciences, and not least in literary theory. Translation often reveals critical points or differences in the two cultures involved, and one just has to go on until one has found a solution. The search for equivalents, or working round the problem, is what teaches us what's going on – what takes us to the centre of the problem itself. Perhaps we could call on my project colleague Guillemette Bolens to tell us how she handles the term 'embodiment', since she has written about this in both French and English.

Guillemette Bolens: Actually, in French, 'embodiment' is now often translated by 'corporalité', precisely because 'incarnation' is too culturally connoted. But in the end I opted for the notion of 'kinesis', precisely because 'embodiment' is immediately associated with cultural ways of conceptualizing the body. By focusing on kinesis, I tried to address gestures, postures, and movements differently, in order to get as close as possible to the literary texts under study. And to answer your specific question, I started writing about kinesis in French. It is not the Anglo-Saxon concepts that made me think about such issues. However, you are right to point out that, had I started thinking in terms of 'incarnation', my research would have been entirely different.

Elleke Boehmer: I have a very short response, a pragmatic response that may help here. When we think about singing or chanting a poem, or singing a song, we can imagine embodiment, the sounds vibrating through us, the throat and mouth as a moving vessel for the song or poem, even though we might not have a suitable word for it – a scientific term, if you like.

Second question from the audience: Well, I was intrigued by your example from Coleridge, where you used the way sounds are articulated to emphasize the kinetic aspect of it. Now I'm wondering to what extent the process of reading aloud, reading silently, the history of these processes plays into your research.

Elleke Boehmer: The focus of the question was on history? How our understanding of both the oral and the literary traditions that Coleridge was appealing to comes into our reading?

Second question from the audience: Two points. One: is silent reading equivalent to articulating aloud? Or are these two different things? And there the history of reading comes in. People did not always read aloud – did not articulate. Do we articulate somehow when we read silently? It does seem to make a difference.

Elleke Boehmer: It does. I agree. It does make a difference. Terence, did you want to come in? I would venture to say that silent reading and reading or speaking literature aloud are different, but related processes. Silent reading is culturally determined in a very marked way. There are many cultures that initially read aloud, or with some sort of sound, which is why I put some emphasis in my opening paragraph on oral cultures. That's one mode of reception for what we call literature. And then there's silent reading, which is linguistically similar in terms of how we process the words, but is different, too, in terms of the seemingly quieter and more static medium of the reception. I think it's very interesting that in "The Rime of the Ancient Mariner", Coleridge was thinking about and adapting the ballad form, which is a sung form. So, even if very residually, there is some sense still of the spoken or the singing voice in the poem. It is palpable all the way through in the ballad-like rhyme scheme, and the somatic, resonantal qualities that Coleridge builds into the poem. Therefore, even if we read the poem silently, we have a shadow, or retain an echo of those oral processes at work.

Terence Cave: I think that, cognitively speaking, the difference between reading silently and reading aloud is in most respects minimal. If I read silently, I probably don't imagine all of the sounds in the way that I have to when I articulate them orally. But I think all the evidence is that actually you do marshal the same motor processes when you read silently as you do when you articulate. That is to say, there is, as Elleke suggested, more than a trace of the muscular and other processes that are involved in articulating the sounds.

Third question from the audience: This is a follow-up question, really, to the one about embodiment, and I wonder if you could very briefly comment on the intersection of cognitive criticism and the question of embodiment as it is looked at in recently emerging affect theory. Is it that maybe the question of embodiment is a potential place of convergence for cognitive approaches and theoretical approaches?

Terence Cave: Well, if I'm going to reply to that, I'm afraid I'll have to ask you to say a bit more about what you understand by affect theory, because often when we use these words, we end up finding that we are talking about different things.

Third question from the audience: Of course...

Terence Cave: This is still quite a fragmented field where people do different things in different places. That's one of the problems.

Third question from the audience: While I was waiting to get the microphone, I was actually racking my brains trying to find out how I would define affect theory. I guess it is... it focuses on the reciprocality of texts structuring bodies and bodies structuring texts. So not only does language have a lot to do with the kinds of beings that we physically are, and we've seen certain examples of that in the poems that both you and Professor Boehmer have discussed, but also texts have an awful lot to do with the kind of bodies that we end up having and experiencing. So if you think, for instance, about the politics that surround disability and how that's been discussed in disability studies, that would be affect theory for me.

Terence Cave: Well, that is certainly a fascinating variant, and a further branch of the area of studies we in our Balzan project are involved in. We haven't done it quite that way, although we are certainly interested in ways in which the world might be embodied for somebody, for example, who is autistic. There are now quite a number of literary representations of people on that spectrum, and they raise complex and delicate issues. But I would have thought that in the end we are going to find that there is a lot of common ground between our approaches. Emotion is an integral part of the way cognition works, so affect, which is a way of thinking about emotion, would certainly play a major role in any cognitive approach to literature and thought.

Fourth question from the audience: You've raised – for me – some very interesting questions about the text that thinks, and I would have loved to have heard Professor Cave talk a little more about scientific literature or other kinds of literature, because I've been a bit worried about defining literature in terms of rhythm, story. It seems to me – and especially the quote from Milton leading you to a thinking mind – John Milton's mind, the author in a vial and so forth. It won't work for certain kinds of texts; it will work for others, and it implies a single author, who is John Milton. And as a medievalist, for example, but not only as a medievalist, I'm working with all kinds of other text types. I don't think that the way that you've been defining the problems would necessarily work for a text that is, say, a multi-text, like Mandeville's *Travels*, which is the result of centuries of accretion, of travel literature from the Franciscans to fifteenth century compendia made up from various authors claiming to represent their own experiences. So we don't have the Miltonic author behind these texts. How comprehensive can you claim to be in your approach? Where would you set the limits to the kinds of things you've been talking about this evening?

Terence Cave: Well, that's a brilliant question, and one that we need to think about a lot. It's obvious, isn't it, that the case is easier for me as I've made it with an author called John Milton whom we can identify, who is speaking in his own name. It's harder for Shakespeare: not everybody thinks Shakespeare is Shakespeare, and there are certainly bits of 'his' texts which may be by somebody else. And as you go further back into European culture, but also of course into other cultures, you have anonymous texts, or texts that might be copied, and so on. I think that that's an interesting challenge. However, I don't think that it defeats the notion that, where a communicative discourse is perceived as distinctive or cognitively powerful, it is heard as the speech of some particular agent, even if that's an anonymous person. For the reader, it is still a discourse that issues from somewhere. That somewhere might be a group: there are in fact modern texts, as well as earlier ones, which are group constructs. So, in a sense, were the poems of 'Homer', but generations of readers have still wanted to give him a name because the voice sounds like an individual voice. But yes, we ought to think more about dealing with those cases because clearly a lot of literature outside the European or Western tradition may be anonymous in various ways, or group products in various ways. In principle, the cognitive approach needs to be able to adjust for those cases because in fact they form the majority of all cases of imaginative speech that one can dream up. After all, you've got to assume that we're also talking here about stories told by people living, say, in 30,000 B.C. However, as I see it, the story or the poem would still be imagined as emerging from a human or perhaps a group of humans who have a particular purpose and a particular cultural agenda: they want to *intervene* in their world in a certain way. And I suspect that the naming of a communicative act, where it is perceived as especially rich or skilful, goes back a very long way: it isn't a modern invention, as is sometimes claimed. Thank you again for that excellent question.

Elleke Boehmer: Just to add a post-script to that. For me, no approach to texts or a text is the single authoritative route; the key to all mythologies. Some texts work better with some approaches than others: practical criticism, for example, applied itself in particularly productive ways to a short lyric poem; a narratological reading might find a layered novel especially rich and interesting. Personally, I'm happy with it that way. I chose those three examples over several others that I was entertaining, because they spoke particularly well within the short period of time I had, to the idea of cognitive reading that Terence was sketching for us. For me, the richness of this approach for my own field – the great richness – is that it allows me to speak about the semantics of form and structure in texts outside Europe in ways that haven't been accessible or allowable till quite recently in the field. In Postcolonial Studies – though I'm generalizing grossly – readings have tended to be informed by particular agendas. We have generally read for something: we have read for race; we've read for resistance. But now, through the cognitive approach, I believe – even though I'm only just edging my way into it – through this approach, we can start thinking about the meaningful work of form, of structure, of rhyme, in any literary work, any piece of crafted imaginative writing, from anywhere, as I was saying; there is no barrier.

Thomas Claviez: While we're at it, I might actually add something to it. Obviously, and you can imagine that as a professor of literary theory, I was grinding my teeth a bit in between. I've been wondering about the surplus value – Elleke mentioned part of it – but it seemed to me that the kind of objections that you have toward literary theory is that it is in one way programmatic, and that it tries to project itself onto the texts, and turn the texts into the allegories of theory, which is something that I always warn my students about – that this is not what I want to see, right? Because otherwise the people would have written not novels, but theory. So why look for a theory in the novel? Thus there's always a dialogue going on, and there's always a rest that theory will never be able to apprehend, so to speak. But talking about cognition, I had the impression that on the one hand, this concept is very general, and that it defines literature as a particular mode of cognition, and I would actually have loved to hear more about the specific form of cognition that literature actually allows, that other discourses don't do, for example, theory. You said that literature in itself provides a certain very ingenious mixture between all those different aspects of cognition. So that's the very general aspect, and then there is a very specific aspect, because it seems to me that the examples that you showed actually showed acts of cognition *in* literature, a certain kind of self-reflexivity of literature about cognition in itself. So on the one hand it's very general; on the other hand, it seems to be very specific in that, as I said, the examples that you mentioned were highly self-reflective, and you can obviously read this as literature that is about, or that is on, cognition. But the question would then be where do we go from there? Is it just a certain self-reflective level in literature, or would we then actually be able to address certain forms of differences, of mis-cognitions, even of de-cognitions, if that were possible?

Terence Cave: Well, there's a lot to talk about there. On the general and the specific, all I can say is that, yes, I begin from the assumption that literature, in the broad sense, provides us with an extraordinary archive and laboratory of cognitively rich utterances; it uses the resources of everyday thinking, feeling, imagining in bold and innovative and demanding ways. Analysing them individually therefore requires the use of an appropriately cognitive instrumentation. And it would certainly include, as you suggest, paying attention to cognitive failures, inhibitions, dissonances.

On the question of 'self-reflexive' examples, yes again, I did choose examples which make salient, make explicit even, a mode of thought – Rebecca Elson's reference to inference, the second stanza of the Marvell example, the scene of reading in *Lord Jim*. That allowed me both to develop my explicit cognitive theme and at the same time to show what a cognitive reading might look like: when one has only 40 minutes to present a whole perspective, one has to make economies. But the cognitive approach doesn't depend on instances of that kind, interesting as they are. I've just completed a book which has a whole range of examples from different genres and historical periods, and in most of them the cognitive analysis passes through features that are not immediately salient – kinesic expressions, or procedural or modalizing expressions like the word "perhaps" in the Conrad fragment.

But I would argue that, even in the examples which make the act of cognition explicit in some way, this is quite unlike the 'self-reflexivity' we all talked about in the 1970s and 1980s, which was the object of a critical or theoretical move designed to undermine naïve assumptions about the representational nature of texts and lay bare their underlying textuality. Crucially, it was aimed at aesthetic or textual self-consciousness, not cognitive self-awareness. It would be interesting, in fact, to re-examine such cases in the light of a cognitive approach – I think you'd get entirely different results. Unfortunately there's not time to do that here.

Elleke Boehmer: I think here of the rather apt example of the writer J.M. Coetzee and of his notebooks, which have recently been put on display in the Henry Ransom Center in Austin, Texas. In these notebooks, he often seems to suggest that novels give him a more mobile medium with which to think than does criticism. Of course, he's written both, fiction and criticism. And of course, the thinking mind at work is very evident throughout the work writing of J.M. Coetzee. But it remains very interesting that he spoke of the novel as a mode through which to think critically. That is what I think Terence is particularly concerned with in his current work.

Thomas Claviez: Thank you very much, Terence Cave and Elleke Boehmer, and my thanks to you all, ladies and gentlemen, for coming today.

View of the city of Berne and surroundings from the University, with the Bernese Alps in the background.

2014 Annual Balzan Lecture, Auditorium Maximum, University of Berne. Above: International Balzan Foundation "Prize" President Enrico Decleva. Below: Co-Director of the Center for Cultural Studies and Director of the University of Berne "World Literature" MA Program Thomas Claviez.

2014 Annual Balzan Lecture, Main Building (Auditorium Maximum), University of Berne. Above: University of Berne President Martin Täuber welcomes the audience. Below: Swiss Academies of Arts and Sciences President Thierry Courvoisier and Balzan Distinguished Lecturer Terence Cave.

2014 Annual Balzan Lecture, Auditorium Maximum, University of Berne. Reception before the beginning of the Lecture.

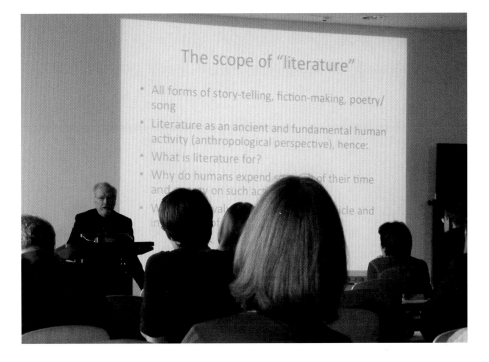

2014 Annual Balzan Lecture, Auditorium Maximum, University of Berne. Above: Balzan Distinguished Lecturer Terence Cave. Below: University of Oxford World Literature Professor and Respondent Professor Elleke Boehmer, Co-Director of the Center for Cultural Studies and Director of the University of Berne "World Literature" MA Program Thomas Claviez and Balzan Distinguished Lecturer Terence Cave.

2014 Annual Balzan Lecture, Auditorium Maximum, University of Berne. Above: Balzan Distinguished Lecturer Terence Cave. Below: Entrance to the Lecture.

BIOGRAPHICAL AND BIBLIOGRAPHICAL DATA

Terence Cave is Emeritus Professor of French Literature in the University of Oxford and Emeritus Research Fellow of St. John's College, Oxford. He has devoted most of his career to teaching and research in the field of early modern French literature, thought and culture. His major publications in this area include *Devotional Poetry in France 1570-1613* (Cambridge University Press, 1969), *The Cornucopian Text: Problems of Writing in the French Renaissance* (Oxford, Clarendon Press, 1979 and reprints; French translation 1997), *Pré-histoires: textes troublés au seuil de la modernité* (Geneva, Droz, 1999), *Pré-histoires II: langues étrangères et troubles économiques au XVIe siècle* (Geneva, Droz, 2001), and *How to Read Montaigne* (London, Granta Books, 2007). He is the editor of *Thomas More's* Utopia *in Early Modern Europe: Paratexts and Contexts* (Manchester University Press, 2008) and other collective volumes, and has translated and edited Madame de Lafayette's *La Princesse de Clèves* and other works for Oxford World's Classics (1992).

However, he has always taken a wider interest in European literature and the history of poetics. His principal contributions in this field include *Recognitions: A Study in Poetics* (Oxford, Clarendon Press, 1988 and reprints) and *Mignon's Afterlives: Crossing Cultures from Goethe to the Twenty-First Century* (Oxford University Press, 2011). He has also published editions of George Eliot's *Daniel Deronda* (Penguin Books, 1995) and *Silas Marner* (Oxford World's Classics, 1996). Together with Sarah Kay and Malcolm Bowie, he is the joint author of *A Short History of French Literature* (Oxford University Press, 2003). He is currently a reader for the new Penguin English translation of Henrik Ibsen's principal plays.

In December 2001, he took early retirement in order to concentrate on research. In 2009 he was awarded the Balzan Foundation

Prize for 'Literature since 1500', and he is currently director of the Balzan Interdisciplinary Seminar 'Literature as an Object of Knowledge', based at the St. John's College Research Centre. In connection with that project, he has recently completed a book, entitled *Thinking with Literature*, on ways of integrating cognitive research into mainstream readings of literature; the book has been accepted for publication by Oxford University Press.

He is Member of the Academia Europaea (1990), Fellow of the British Academy (1991), Member of the Royal Norwegian Society of Science and Letters, Trondheim (1993), Honorary Fellow of Gonville and Caius College, Cambridge (1997), Chevalier dans l'Ordre National du Mérite (2001), Honorary DLit, University of London (2007), Commander of the Order of the British Empire (2013), and Foreign Member of the Norwegian Academy of Science and Letters.

THE BALZAN INTERDISCIPLINARY SEMINAR: LITERATURE AS AN OBJECT OF KNOWLEDGE

Adviser for the Balzan General Prize Committee: Karlheinz Stierle

Terence Cave has used the second half of his Balzan Prize to explore the value of literature as an object of knowledge, and more specifically, the cognitive value of literature in relation to other kinds of discourse. The research project is based at the Research Centre of St. John's College, Oxford. The word "seminar" is used in the title to indicate the heuristic nature of the project: the core of the work lies in discussions designed to foster a sharper awareness of the issues that are at stake and to explore new directions in the understanding of literature.

The collective work of the project was carried out for the most part in workshops and discussion groups in which interdisciplinary issues were explored and debated with the cooperation of colleagues from non-literary disciplines. The twin themes of knowledge and cognition provided a focus for the discussions. The integrity of individual research programmes was respected, but they were also used as test-cases or illustrations of the broader interdisciplinary issues raised by the project.

Two Balzan Postdoctoral Research Fellowships were established at the outset of the project, tenable for 3 years. The Research Fellows were expected to produce published work of the equivalent of a book-length study over the course of their Fellowship. They also assisted in the arrangement of discussion groups, workshops and other collective events. They were not permitted to take on duties external to the project (for example teaching duties) except with the agreement of the Director. The Research Fellowships were attached to the St. John's College Research Centre in Oxford, where the Fellows had offices.

Five Balzan Research Lectureships were conferred on younger colleagues holding permanent academic positions at five different UK universities, each lasting up to one semester on a "buy-out" basis. The positions carried with them the obligation to produce at least one article-length publication during the period of leave, and (under the guidance of the Director) to arrange a two-day workshop at the end of the period of leave structured around the Lecturer's work. The Research Lecturers were expected to participate as far as their other duties permitted in the other collective activities of the project. The workshops were held in the lecturer's home institution; this arrangement helped to guarantee the wider diffusion of the project's aims and intellectual outcomes.

The project also recruited a number of Associate Researchers. This group consisted of individual researchers from various academic contexts whose work was closely related to the aims of the project. They had no specific duties, but were expected to attend workshops and discussion groups in their areas of interest.

A discussion group, consisting of core project members and other invited participants from the University of Oxford (academic post-holders, postdoctoral researchers, and a small number of doctoral students) was established in Oxford for the duration of the project. It met about once a month to discuss specific topics and problems arising from the project's aim to develop a cognitive methodology for the study of literature. Visiting speakers with relevant interests were sometimes invited to give presentations to the group. The two Balzan Postdoctoral Fellows organized one-day workshops of their own in the final year of their tenure (2012-13). In addition, the project provided intellectual support and limited financial support for workshops on relevant topics organized by its Associate Researchers.

A programme of individual visits and exchange visits enabled core project participants to establish appropriate contacts in other universities, with the possibility of reciprocation. In addition, the Director gave (and continues to give) public lectures both in the UK and abroad and actively seeks to create an interdisciplinary network that will not only support and enhance the work of the project but also ensure that its intellectual energies are propagated beyond the lifetime of the project itself.

The first phase of the project ended on 30 September 2013, with a Methodological Colloquium entitled "Thinking with Literature" from

9 to 12 September 2013 at the University of Oslo, Centre for the Study of Mind in Nature, and ILOS (organised by Kirsti Sellevold, Terence Cave, Karin Kukkonen and Olivia Smith).

Further workshops and publications are currently in progress, and will continue while funds remain.

BOOK-LENGTH PUBLICATIONS:

CAVE, TERENCE, KARIN KUKKONEN and OLIVIA SMITH, eds. "Reading Literature Cognitively." *Paragraph* 37.1 (March 2014, includes contributions by ten members of the project team).

FORTHCOMING OR IN PROGRESS:

CARACCIOLO, MARCO and KARIN KUKKONEN, eds. "Second-Generation Cognitive Approaches to Literature." *Style* 48 (2015, forthcoming).

CAVE, TERENCE. *Thinking with Literature: Towards a Cognitively Inflected Criticism.* (Oxford University Press, forthcoming).

KUKKONEN, KARIN. *A Prehistory of Cognitive Poetics: Neoclassicism and the Novel.* (complete and under consideration for publication).

MAC CARTHY, ITA, KIRSTI SELLEVOLD and OLIVIA SMITH, eds. *Cognitive Confusions: Dreams, Delusions and Illusions in Early Modern Culture.* (Oxford: Legenda, forthcoming).

SMITH, OLIVIA. *Inside the Furnished Mind: A Literary Reading of Locke's* Essay. (nearing completion).

PROFILES

THE INTERNATIONAL BALZAN FOUNDATION

The *International Balzan Foundation "Prize"* aims to promote, throughout the world, culture, science, and the most meritorious initiatives in the cause of humanity, peace and fraternity among peoples, regardless of nationality, race or creed. This aim is attained through the annual award of prizes in two general academic categories: literature, the moral sciences and the arts; medicine and the physical, mathematical and natural sciences. Specific subjects for the awarding of Prizes are chosen on an annual basis.

Nominations for these prizes are received at the Foundation's request from the world's leading academic institutions. Candidates are selected by the *General Prize Committee*, composed of eminent European scholars and scientists. Prizewinners must allocate half of the Prize to research work, preferably involving young researchers.

At intervals of not less than three years, the Balzan Foundation also awards a prize of varying amounts for Humanity, Peace and Fraternity among Peoples.

The *International Balzan Foundation "Prize"* attains its financial means from the *International Balzan Foundation "Fund"* which administers Eugenio Balzan's estate.

THE SWISS ACADEMIES OF ARTS AND SCIENCES

The Association of the *Swiss Academies of Arts and Sciences* includes the Swiss Academy of Sciences (SCNAT), the Swiss Academy of Humanities and Social Sciences (SAHS), the Swiss Academy of Medical Sciences (SAMS), and the Swiss Academy of Engineering Sciences (SATW) as well as the two Centres for Excellence TA-SWISS and Science et Cité. Their collaboration is focused on methods of anticipating future trends, ethics and the dialogue between science, the arts and society. It is the aim of the *Swiss Academies of Arts and Sciences* to develop an equal dialogue between academia and society and to advise Government on scientifically based, socially relevant questions. The academies stand for an open and pluralistic understanding of science and the arts. Over the long-term, they mutually commit to resolving interdisciplinary questions in the following areas:

– They offer knowledge and expertise in relation to socially relevant subjects in the fields of Education, Research and Technology.
– They adhere to the concept of ethically-based responsibility in gaining and applying scientific and humanistic knowledge.
– They build bridges between Academia, Government and Society.

THE ACCADEMIA NAZIONALE DEI LINCEI

The *Accademia Nazionale dei Lincei*, founded in 1603 by the Roman-Umbrian aristocrat Federico Cesi and three other young scholars, Anastasio De Filiis, Johannes Eck and Francesco Stelluti, is the oldest scientific academy in the world. It promotes academic excellence through its Fellows whose earliest members included, among many other renowned names, Galileo Galilei.

The Academy's mission is "to promote, coordinate, integrate and disseminate scientific knowledge in its highest expressions in the context of cultural unity and universality".

The activities of the Academy are carried out according to two guiding principles that complement one another: to enrich academic knowledge and disseminate the fruits of this. To this end, the Accademia Nazionale dei Lincei organises national and international conferences, meetings and seminars, and encourages academic cooperation and exchange between scientists and scholars at the national and international level. The Academy promotes research activities and missions, confers awards and grants, publishes the reports of its own sessions and the notes and records presented therein, as well as the proceedings of its conferences, meetings and seminars.

The Academy further provides – either upon request or on its own initiative – advice to public institutions and drafts relevant reports when appropriate. Since 1992, the Academy has served as an official adviser to the President of the Italian Republic in relation to scholarly and scientific matters.

AGREEMENTS ON COLLABORATION BETWEEN
THE INTERNATIONAL BALZAN FOUNDATION "PRIZE",
THE SWISS ACADEMIES OF ARTS AND SCIENCES
AND THE ACCADEMIA NAZIONALE DEI LINCEI
(Hereafter referred to as the 'Balzan', the 'Swiss Academies' and the 'Lincei', respectively)

The main points of the agreements between the Balzan, the Swiss Academies and the Lincei are the following:

1) The promotion of the Balzan Prize and the presentation of the Prizewinners through the academies' channels of communication, in Italy and Switzerland as well as abroad. By virtue of the relations of the Swiss Academies and the Lincei with academies of other countries and with international academic organizations, they will contribute to more widespread circulation of news related to the Balzan;

2) On the occasion of the Awards ceremony of the Balzan Prize, held on alternating years in Berne and Rome, each academy will contribute to the academic organization of an interdisciplinary Forum, in the course of which the Prizewinners of that year will present their academic work and discuss it with other academics proposed by the academies. Furthermore, in the years when the ceremony is held in Rome, one of the Prizewinners will give the Balzan Annual Lecture in Switzerland, and when the ceremony is held in Berne, the Balzan Annual Lecture will be organized at the headquarters of the Lincei in Rome;

3) The academies will contribute to a series of publications in English (ideally with summaries in Italian, German and French), created by the Balzan, with the collaboration of the Balzan Prizewinners.

To promote and supervise all these initiatives, two Commissions have been set up, one between the Balzan and the Swiss Academies, and the other between the Balzan and the Lincei. Both commissions are chaired by Professor Alberto Quadrio Curzio as a representative of the Balzan, while the Balzan Secretary General, Dr. Suzanne Werder, has been appointed Secretary of both Commissions.

THE BALZAN FOUNDATION "PRIZE"

BOARD

(December 2014)

ALBERTO DEVOTO

Member
Professor in the Physics Department of the University of Cagliari; former Scientific Attaché of the Embassy of Italy in Washington; appointed by an interministerial decree of the Italian Ministry of Foreign Affairs and Ministry of Education, Universities and Research as Representative of the Italian Republic on the Balzan Foundation "Prize" Board

PAOLO MATTHIAE

Member
Professor Emeritus of Archaeology and History of Art of the Ancient Near East at the University of Rome "La Sapienza"; Fellow of the Accademia Nazionale dei Lincei, Rome; appointed by the Balzan General Prize Committee as their Representative on the Balzan Foundation "Prize" Board

GENERAL PRIZE COMMITTEE

(December 2014)

SALVATORE VECA	*Chairman* Professor of Political Philosophy at the Institute for Advanced Study (IUSS), Pavia
ENRIC BANDA	*Vice Chairman* Research Professor of Geophysics at the Institute of Earth Sciences in Barcelona, Spanish Council for Scientific Research (CSIC); former Secretary General of the European Science Foundation, Strasbourg; Member of the Academia Europaea and of the Barcelona Royal Academy of Sciences and Arts
PAOLO MATTHIAE	*Vice Chairman* Professor Emeritus of Archaeology and History of Art of the Ancient Near East at the University of Rome "La Sapienza"; Fellow of the Accademia Nazionale dei Lincei, Rome
ETIENNE GHYS	*Member* Research Director at the Centre National de la Recherche Scientifique, Pure and Applied Mathematics Unit, École Normale Supérieure de Lyon; Member of the Académie des sciences, Institut de France, Paris
H. CHARLES J. GODFRAY	*Member* Hope Professor of Zoology at the University of Oxford and Fellow of Jesus College; Fellow of the Royal Society
BENGT GUSTAFSSON	*Member* Professor Emeritus of Theoretical Astrophysics at the University of Uppsala; Member of the Royal Swedish Academy of Sciences, the Royal Danish Academy of Sciences and Letters, and the Norwegian Academy of Science and Letters

JULES A. HOFFMANN

Member
Professor at the Institut d'Études Avancées at the University of Strasbourg; former President of the Académie des sciences, Institut de France, Paris; 2011 Nobel Prize for Physiology or Medicine

LUCIANO MAIANI

Member
Professor Emeritus of Theoretical Physics at the University of Rome "La Sapienza"; Fellow of the Accademia Nazionale dei Lincei, Rome, and of the American Physical Society

THOMAS MAISSEN

Member
Director of the German Historical Institute in Paris; Chair in Early Modern History at the University of Heidelberg; Member of the Heidelberger Akademie der Wissenschaften

ERWIN NEHER

Member
Professor Emeritus, Max Planck Institute for Biophysical Chemistry, Göttingen; Member of the Academia Europaea; Foreign Associate of the US National Academy of Sciences and of the Royal Society, London; 1991 Nobel Prize for Physiology or Medicine

ANTONIO PADOA SCHIOPPA

Member
Professor Emeritus of Legal History at the University of Milan; former President of the Istituto Lombardo, Academy of Sciences and the Humanities, Milan; Corresponding Foreign Fellow of the Académie des inscriptions et belles-lettres, Institut de France, Paris

DOMINIQUE SCHNAPPER

Member
Research Director at the École des hautes études en sciences sociales (EHESS), Paris; Honorary Member of the French Conseil Constitutionnel; Foreign Fellow of the Accademia Nazionale dei Lincei, Rome

GOTTFRIED SCHOLZ

Member
Professor Emeritus of Music Analysis at the University of Music and Performing Arts, Vienna; Fellow of the Sudetendeutsche Akademie der Wissenschaften und Künste, Munich

CLAUDIO GENERALI

Member
Former Member of the Governing Council of the Canton of Ticino, responsible for finances and public works; former President of the Association of Foreign Banks in Switzerland and former Vice President of Swiss Radio and Television RTS; Chairman of the Ticino Banking Association

ARINA KOWNER

Member
Lawyer; Cultural Entrepreneur: promotion and representation of Russian culture; Collector of contemporary Russian art; Book "Passion Picture"; Member of the Paul Sacher Foundation; former Board Member of Pro Helvetia and former Member of the Swiss UNESCO committee

BALZAN PRIZEWINNERS
FOR LITERATURE, MORAL SCIENCES, AND THE ARTS;
FOR PHYSICAL, MATHEMATICAL
AND NATURAL SCIENCES, AND MEDICINE

2014

    IAN HACKING (Canada) Epistemology and Philosophy of Mind
    DAVID TILMAN (USA) Basic/applied Plant Ecology
    DENNIS SULLIVAN (USA) Mathematics (pure/applied)
    MARIO TORELLI (Italy) Classical Archaeology

2013

    ALAIN ASPECT (France) Quantum Information Processing and
        Communication
    MANUEL CASTELLS (USA/Catalonia) Sociology
    PASCALE COSSART (France) Infectious Diseases: basic and clinical aspects
    ANDRÉ VAUCHEZ (France) Medieval History

2012

    DAVID CHARLES BAULCOMBE (UK) Epigenetics
    RONALD M. DWORKIN (USA) Jurisprudence
    KURT LAMBECK (Australia/The Netherlands) Solid Earth Sciences, with
        emphasis on interdisciplinary research
    REINHARD STROHM (UK/Germany) Musicology

2011

    BRONISLAW BACZKO (Switzerland/Poland) Enlightenment Studies
    PETER ROBERT LAMONT BROWN (USA/Ireland) Ancient History (The
        Graeco-Roman World)
    RUSSELL SCOTT LANDE (UK/USA) Theoretical Biology or Bioinformatics
    JOSEPH IVOR SILK (USA/UK) The Early Universe (From the Planck Time to
        the First Galaxies)

2010

    MANFRED BRAUNECK (Germany) The History of Theatre in All Its Aspects
    CARLO GINZBURG (Italy) European History (1400-1700)

JACOB PALIS (Brazil) Mathematics (pure and applied)
SHINYA YAMANAKA (Japan) Stem Cells: Biology and Potential Applications

2009

TERENCE CAVE (UK) Literature since 1500
MICHAEL GRÄTZEL (Switzerland/Germany) The Science of New Materials
BRENDA MILNER (Canada/UK) Cognitive Neurosciences
PAOLO ROSSI MONTI (Italy) History of Science

2008

WALLACE S. BROECKER (USA) The Science of Climate Change
MAURIZIO CALVESI (Italy) The Visual Arts since 1700
IAN H. FRAZER (Australia/UK) Preventive Medicine
THOMAS NAGEL (USA/Serbia) Moral Philosophy

2007

ROSALYN HIGGINS (UK) International Law since 1945
SUMIO IIJIMA (Japan) Nanoscience
MICHEL ZINK (France) European Literature (1000-1500)
BRUCE BEUTLER (USA) and JULES HOFFMANN (France/Luxembourg)
    Innate Immunity

2006

LUDWIG FINSCHER (Germany) History of Western Music since 1600
QUENTIN SKINNER (UK) Political Thought; History and Theory
PAOLO DE BERNARDIS (Italy) and ANDREW LANGE (USA) Observational
    Astronomy and Astrophysics
ELLIOT MEYEROWITZ (USA) and CHRISTOPHER SOMERVILLE (USA/Canada)
    Plant Molecular Genetics

2005

PETER HALL (UK) The Social and Cultural History of Cities since the
    Beginning of the 16th Century
LOTHAR LEDDEROSE (Germany) The History of the Art of Asia
PETER and ROSEMARY GRANT (USA/UK) Population Biology
RUSSELL HEMLEY (USA) and HO-KWANG MAO (USA/China) Mineral Physics

2004

PIERRE DELIGNE (USA/Belgium) Mathematics
NIKKI RAGOZIN KEDDIE (USA) The Islamic World from the End of the
    19th to the End of the 20th Century
MICHAEL MARMOT (UK) Epidemiology
COLIN RENFREW (UK) Prehistoric Archaeology

2003

REINHARD GENZEL (Germany) Infrared Astronomy
ERIC HOBSBAWM (UK/Egypt) European History since 1900
WEN-HSIUNG LI (USA/Taiwan) Genetics and Evolution
SERGE MOSCOVICI (France/Romania) Social Psychology

2002

WALTER JAKOB GEHRING (Switzerland) Developmental Biology
ANTHONY THOMAS GRAFTON (USA) History of the Humanities
XAVIER LE PICHON (France/Vietnam) Geology
DOMINIQUE SCHNAPPER (France) Sociology

2001

JAMES SLOSS ACKERMAN (USA) History of Architecture
JEAN-PIERRE CHANGEUX (France) Cognitive Neurosciences
MARC FUMAROLI (France) Literary History and Criticism (post 1500)
CLAUDE LORIUS (France) Climatology

2000

ILKKA HANSKI (Finland) Ecological Sciences
MICHEL MAYOR (Switzerland) Instrumentation and Techniques in
    Astronomy and Astrophysics
MICHAEL STOLLEIS (Germany) Legal History since 1500
MARTIN LITCHFIELD WEST (UK) Classical Antiquity

1999

LUIGI LUCA CAVALLI-SFORZA (USA/Italy) The Science of Human Origins
JOHN ELLIOTT (UK) History, 1500-1800
MIKHAEL GROMOV (France/Russia) Mathematics
PAUL RICŒUR (France) Philosophy

1998

HARMON CRAIG (USA) Geochemistry
ROBERT MCCREDIE MAY (UK/Australia) Biodiversity
ANDRZEJ WALICKI (USA/Poland) The Cultural and Social History of the
    Slavonic World

1997

CHARLES COULSTON GILLISPIE (USA) History and Philosophy of Science
THOMAS WILSON MEADE (UK) Epidemiology
STANLEY JEYARAJA TAMBIAH (USA/Sri Lanka) Social Sciences: Social
    Anthropology

1996

ARNO BORST (Germany) History: Medieval Cultures
ARNT ELIASSEN (Norway) Meteorology
STANLEY HOFFMANN (France/USA/Austria) Political Science: Contemporary
  International Relations

1995

YVES BONNEFOY (France) Art History and Art Criticism
CARLO M. CIPOLLA (Italy) Economic History
ALAN J. HEEGER (USA) The Science of New Non-Biological Materials

1994

NORBERTO BOBBIO (Italy) Law and Political Science
RENÉ COUTEAUX (France) Biology
FRED HOYLE (UK) and MARTIN SCHWARZSCHILD (USA/Germany) Astrophysics

1993

WOLFGANG H. BERGER (USA/Germany) Palaeontology with special
  reference to Oceanography
LOTHAR GALL (Germany) History: Societies of the 19th and 20th Centuries
JEAN LECLANT (France) Art and Archaeology of the Ancient World

1992

ARMAND BOREL (USA/Switzerland) Mathematics
GIOVANNI MACCHIA (Italy) History and Criticism of Literature
EBRAHIM M. SAMBA (Gambia) Preventive Medicine

1991

GYÖRGY LIGETI (Austria/Hungary/Romania) Music
VITORINO MAGALHÃES GODINHO (Portugal) History: The Emergence of
  Europe in the 15th and 16th Centuries
JOHN MAYNARD SMITH (UK) Genetics and Evolution

1990

WALTER BURKERT (Switzerland/Germany) The Study of the Ancient World
JAMES FREEMAN GILBERT (USA) Geophysics
PIERRE LALIVE D'EPINAY (Switzerland) Private International Law

1989

EMMANUEL LÉVINAS (France/Lithuania) Philosophy
LEO PARDI (Italy) Ethology
MARTIN JOHN REES (UK) High Energy Astrophysics

1988

SHMUEL NOAH EISENSTADT (Israel/Poland) Sociology
RENÉ ÉTIEMBLE (France) Comparative Literature
MICHAEL EVENARI (Israel/France) and OTTO LUDWIG LANGE (Germany)
   Applied Botany

1987

JEROME SEYMOUR BRUNER (USA) Human Psychology
RICHARD W. SOUTHERN (UK) Medieval History
PHILLIP V. TOBIAS (South Africa) Physical Anthropology

1986

OTTO NEUGEBAUER (USA/Austria) History of Science
ROGER REVELLE (USA) Oceanography/Climatology
JEAN RIVERO (France) Basic Human Rights

1985

ERNST H.J. GOMBRICH (UK/Austria) History of Western Art
JEAN-PIERRE SERRE (France) Mathematics

1984

JAN HENDRIK OORT (The Netherlands) Astrophysics
JEAN STAROBINSKI (Switzerland) History and Criticism of Literature
SEWALL WRIGHT (USA) Genetics

1983

FRANCESCO GABRIELI (Italy) Oriental Studies
ERNST MAYR (USA/Germany) Zoology
EDWARD SHILS (USA) Sociology

1982

JEAN-BAPTISTE DUROSELLE (France) Social Sciences
MASSIMO PALLOTTINO (Italy) Studies of Antiquity
KENNETH VIVIAN THIMANN (USA/UK) Pure and Applied Botany

1981

JOSEF PIEPER (Germany) Philosophy
PAUL REUTER (France) International Public Law
DAN PETER MCKENZIE, DRUMMOND HOYLE MATTHEWS and
   FREDERICK JOHN VINE (UK) Geology and Geophysics

1980

>   ENRICO BOMBIERI (USA/Italy) Mathematics
>   JORGE LUIS BORGES (Argentina) Philology, Linguistics and Literary Criticism
>   HASSAN FATHY (Egypt) Architecture and Urban Planning

1979

>   TORBJÖRN CASPERSSON (Sweden) Biology
>   JEAN PIAGET (Switzerland) Social and Political Science
>   ERNEST LABROUSSE (France) and GIUSEPPE TUCCI (Italy) History

1962

>   PAUL HINDEMITH (Germany) Music
>   ANDREJ KOLMOGOROV (Russia) Mathematics
>   SAMUEL ELIOT MORISON (USA) History
>   KARL VON FRISCH (Austria) Biology

BALZAN PRIZEWINNERS
FOR HUMANITY, PEACE AND FRATERNITY
AMONG PEOPLES

2014 Association VIVRE EN FAMILLE (France), the creation of a maternity unit and the revitalization of a school in Ibambi in the Democratic Republic of the Congo (DRC)

2007 KARLHEINZ BÖHM (Austria/Germany), Organisation *Menschen für Menschen*, Aid for Ethiopia

2004 COMMUNITY OF SANT'EGIDIO, DREAM programme combating AIDS and malnutrition in Mozambique

2000 ABDUL SATTAR EDHI (Pakistan/India)

1996 INTERNATIONAL COMMITTEE OF THE RED CROSS, endeavours in the hospitals of Wazir Akbar Khan and Karte Seh in Kabul, Afghanistan

1991 ABBÉ PIERRE (France)

1986 UNITED NATIONS REFUGEE AGENCY

1978 MOTHER TERESA OF CALCUTTA (India/Macedonia)

1962 H.H. JOHN XXIII (Vatican City/Italy)

1961 NOBEL FOUNDATION

FINITO DI STAMPARE
PER CONTO DI LEO S. OLSCHKI EDITORE
PRESSO ABC TIPOGRAFIA • SESTO FIORENTINO (FI)
NEL MESE DI OTTOBRE 2015

THE ANNUAL BALZAN LECTURE

1. *The Evolution of Darwin's Finches, Mockingbirds and Flies*, by Peter and Rosemary Grant. 2010.

2. *Humanists with Inky Fingers. The Culture of Correction in Renaissance Europe*, by Anthony Thomas Grafton. 2011.

3. *Cognitive Archaeology from Theory to Practice: The Early Cycladic Sanctuary at Keros*, by Colin Renfrew. 2012.

4. *Fair Society, Healthy Lives*, by Michael Marmot. 2013.

5. *Of Moon and Land, Ice and Strand: Sea Level during Glacial Cycles*, by Kurt Lambeck. 2014.

6. *"Far other worlds, and other seas": Thinking with Literature in the Twenty-First Century*, by Terence Cave. 2015.